Getting Free

Getting Free

How to Move Beyond Conditioning and Be Happy

GINA LAKE

Endless Satsang Foundation

Endless Satsang Foundation

www.radicalhappiness.com

Cover art: © Herzlinde Vancura/Dreamstime.com

ISBN: 978-0-6151-6338-3

Copyright © 2007 by Gina Lake

All rights reserved. No part of this book may be used or reproduced by any means, graphic, electronic, or mechanical, including photocopying, recording, taping, or by any information storage retrieval system without the written permission of the publisher except in the case of brief quotations embodied in critical articles and reviews.

CONTENTS

ACKNOWLEDGMENTS   vii

INTRODUCTION   ix

CHAPTER 1: Understanding Conditioning   1

Why Healing Conditioning Is Necessary—The Role Conditioning Plays in Evolution—The Different Types of Conditioning—What Keeps Conditioning in Place—Trusting that Life Is Good

CHAPTER 2: Experiencing Essence   21

Seeing Radiance—Being Radiant—Moving from the Ego to Essence—Seeing from Essence's Eyes—Love is Your Nature—Every Act Is an Act of Love—Love is All Around—Attention—Acceptance

CHAPTER 3: Healing Conditioning with Positive Thoughts   43

Trusting the Heart—Identifying Negative Beliefs—Replacing Negative Beliefs with Positive Ones—Healing Conditioning in Relationships—When Positive Beliefs Are Not Helpful

CHAPTER 4: Ask and You Shall Receive   67

Help Is Available—An Explanation of Evil—How Negative Nonphysical Beings Affect Humanity—Asking for Help

CHAPTER 5: Clearing Negativity — 85

Clearing Entities—Working with Angels—Untangling Emotional Complexes—Clearing Negative Self-Images—Clearing Negative Thoughts

CHAPTER 6: Using Past-Life Regression to Heal — 113

The Benefits of Past-Life Regression—Who Can Benefit from Past-Life Regression—What to Expect—Hypnosis and Light Trance—An Induction for Past-Life Regression—Healing Traumatic Deaths or Violence—Healing Phobias—Re-scripting—Achieving Essence's Perspective—Coming Out of the Regression

CHAPTER 7: Tools for Moving from the Ego to Essence — 137

Love Heals—Meditation—Prayer—Forgiveness—Gratitude—The Willingness to Not Know—Being Present

ABOUT THE AUTHOR — 161

ACKNOWLEDGMENTS

This book would not have been possible without the help of my inner teacher. It is the result of a collaboration between the wisdom of this teacher and my knowledge, training, understanding, and experience.

INTRODUCTION

Suffering is inherent in the human condition, but freedom from suffering is possible. We are programmed to see ourselves as human, when in fact, our true nature is divine. How we see ourselves is what needs to be healed. Our narrow identity as a human being keeps us tied to suffering and is the cause of suffering. To see ourselves as that which we are not is to live a lie, and that lie can't lead to happiness. We are here to discover who we really are and claim the happiness that is natural to us as the divine expressions of life that we are.

We all have a part to play in the evolution of earth and of humanity, and it may require waking up out of the egoic trance and living from a greater truth. Before you can do that, some healing may be necessary. This book was written to help you free yourself from any limiting beliefs. For that, being open to the possibility that freedom from your conditioning is possible in this lifetime will be helpful. The belief that it isn't possible may be the biggest hurdle of all. Believe that you can be free and be willing to experience that.

This is a simple formula, but it isn't so easy to apply because the mind is a formidable opponent to freedom. It was designed to keep you thinking of yourself the way you do. Getting free requires a new way of thinking or, rather, not thinking. To a large extent, healing our emotional selves is about changing our relationship to our mind and discovering our true nature. This book will help you do that.

Getting free from your conditioning is not only for your own happiness, but also for everyone else's because we are here to serve each other. Getting free is something we do for all of humanity because humanity isn't separate from our own true self. Once the blocks to experiencing our true nature are removed, we can share ourselves with the world in the unique way that we were meant to.

Healing happens when we experience our true self, but to do that we have to become very familiar with the false self and its mistaken beliefs: Before we can discover what is true and live as that, we first have to see what is false and stop believing it. This investigation is something only you can do for yourself, and it isn't always easy. This journey of discovery begins as a solitary one that requires some effort and diligence but ends in the experience of unity with all and true happiness. It is a journey we all eventually take.

CHAPTER 1

Understanding Conditioning

WHY HEALING CONDITIONING IS NECESSARY

Some conditioning is necessary. We need some of it to function, but we don't need all of it. Some of our conditioning keeps us from being happy and finding fulfillment. That is the conditioning that needs healing, or at least, is best ignored. However, even this conditioning serves a purpose in our evolution and growth.

As soon as we come into life, we begin acquiring conditioning. As soon as we are born, our parents and others begin teaching us about life, either intentionally or unintentionally, and we take in what they teach us. Like a sponge, we absorb what we experience in our environment and learn from it. Some of what we are taught and what we learn is useful, necessary, and true (at least some of the time), but much of it is not.

Even before we have a capacity to understand language, we learn from the environment. As infants, we draw certain conclusions that may or may not be correct. Often they are not correct. The conclusions we draw as infants and children are usually narrow representations of what is true about a situation, and they are often unconscious. For example, if as an infant you were hooked up to tubes to keep you alive, you may have concluded that you are weak and powerless, or you may have concluded that the world is frightening and dangerous and that you are very vulnerable. You didn't realize that the tubes actually represented how much people loved you and valued your life. Your conclusion actually didn't represent reality very fully or truly.

Children, and to some extent adults, draw negative or incorrect conclusions about their experience all the time, and these conclusions determine how they respond to their environment. These mistaken or narrow conclusions are part of our conditioning, and they need healing because they interfere with responding to life as it presents itself in each moment. Instead, we respond according to an idea (conditioning) from the past. For example, if an experience caused you to conclude that men with mustaches are mean, then when you encounter someone with a mustache, you'll respond to him as if that were true. You will see meanness even if it isn't there, and you might evoke or provoke it by your prejudicial attitude.

Most of us also have conditioning from our previous lifetimes that interferes in the same way, and those mistaken beliefs also need healing. Conditioning from previous lifetimes operates just like conditioning acquired in the current life, and it is often more powerful. It may have been reinforced over many lifetimes, or the experience that created it may have been so traumatic that the conclusions that were made as a result of that trauma feel very true, even though they aren't true at all. This can be some of the most difficult conditioning to heal.

Much of our negative conditioning came from outside ourselves, that is, it was given to us by others and wasn't the result of conclusions we came to. When we are young, we believe what we are told by our parents and others we are dependent on. We trust them to tell us the truth about the world and ourselves, and we accept what they tell us as true. Unfortunately, much of what they tell us is either not true at all or only true some of the time. When we are young, we aren't able to evaluate what we are told, so if we are told to believe something or if others around us believe something, then that belief is incorporated into our belief system until we are old enough to evaluate our beliefs ourselves. Still, some of our beliefs are never questioned, and many remain unconscious and outside our awareness, where they are safe from scrutiny but still drive us in detrimental ways.

If the beliefs you were given as a child were primarily positive ones (e.g., "You are a good person." "You can do anything you apply yourself to." "Life is meaningful and supportive."), then those beliefs are likely to serve you and help you cope with life. If, on the other hand, your conditioning was primarily negative (e.g. "You can't do anything right." You'll never amount to anything." "People are bad." "Life is always going to disappoint you."), then those beliefs are likely to interfere with trying new things, taking advantage of opportunities, getting along with others, and being happy. Positive conditioning helps us cope with life, while negative conditioning, conditioning that causes us to see life as bad or frightening and ourselves as bad or impotent, not only doesn't help us cope with life, but also makes it difficult to cope with life.

The more negative conditioning you have, the more difficult life will be; and the more positive conditioning you have, the easier life will be. This is because positive conditioning creates a positive mind and feelings, which generally produce and attract positive results in the world, while negative conditioning creates a negative mind and feelings, which generally produce and attract negative results in the world.

A negative mind results in a vicious cycle: Negative thoughts lead to negative feelings, which lead to more negative thoughts and feelings. Negative thoughts make you feel angry, sad, jealous, guilty, hateful, resentful, bitter, and unhappy, and then you feel bad about yourself for having those feelings. That leads to more negative self-talk and more negative feelings, all of which can block you from fulfilling your potential. Fortunately, positive thoughts do the opposite: They create positive feelings and a positive feedback loop. Positive thoughts make you feel good, strong, competent, kind, loving, and supported. Feeling that way makes you feel good about yourself, which produces more positive self-talk and positive feelings and less self-blocking. Here is an exercise that will help you examine your conditioning:

Exercise: Examining Your Conditioning

Make a list of some of the conclusions you have about yourself, others, and life. To help you get started, write: "I am...," "Others are...," and "Life is..." and fill in the blank with as many statements as you can think of. For each statement, ask, "Is that true?" You may believe that it is true, but is it absolutely true of yourself, others, and life? If you can find even one contradictory example, then it isn't true. Another test would be if everyone in the universe agrees that it is true. Add more statements to this list as you discover them.

Becoming aware of what you believe is the first step in freeing yourself from mistaken and counterproductive beliefs. You will discover that you have been allowing many untrue or partially true beliefs to define you and shape your life, your experience, and your interactions with others. Partially true beliefs just aren't that useful. They aren't good guides for how to live your life.

How you feel about yourself and about life has a big impact on how you respond to life and on how life responds back. That's why your conditioning matters so much. Your conditioned beliefs determine your experience of life: When your beliefs are positive, you experience life positively; when your beliefs are negative, you experience life negatively. This is how it is until we begin to wake up to the fact that our conditioning is determining our reactions and behavior, and it doesn't have to. Getting free of our conditioning is a two-fold task: We can free ourselves from our negative beliefs by reprogramming our mind with positive beliefs. We can also get free by seeing that all of our beliefs are just conditioning and that that conditioning doesn't have to be what determines our actions and reactions.

Something else besides conditioning is propelling your life forward, and its actions aren't based on thoughts or on conditioning. You are a spiritual being who is programmed to behave like a human being, with all sorts of conditioning. However, the spiritual being that you are functions perfectly fine without most of your conditioning, particularly your beliefs. The spiritual being that you are moves you, breathes you, inspires you, and communicates through you. It acts and speaks in your life, and when it does that, those actions and speech feel right, true, and fulfilling.

The *you* that you usually think of yourself as, on the other hand, is created by the mind. This *you* is really just thoughts about you: "I like...." "I want...." "I hope...." "I am...." "I was...." "I need...." "I feel...." These thoughts about you give you a sense of self and the impression that you exist as the person you think you are. But, really, you are a spiritual being masquerading as the self that you think of yourself as. The self that is made up of ideas about yourself is the *false self*. It only exists as *ideas*. The true self is all that is really here and all that has ever been here, but the true self allows you to believe that you are the false self.

This masquerade enables the spiritual being that you are to have the experience of being human. You get to try on being this character, and because this character feels so real to you, you experience very intense emotions. You become identified with this character so deeply that you believe you are that character. Masquerading in this way is the only way the spiritual being that you are can have a full experience of being human. Nevertheless, there's a point in everyone's evolution when it is time to wake up from this illusion and remember who you really are. You are probably at this place now or you wouldn't be reading this.

Negative conditioning keeps you identified with the character you are playing because it keeps you involved with negative thoughts and feelings and with trying to fix those thoughts and feelings. When you are deeply involved with negative thoughts and feelings, there's little opportunity to experience your true nature. You believe you are small, weak, unkind, and powerless, and in that state of mind, it's difficult to grasp the truth about who you are. You're too busy trying to think and act your way out of the unhappy situation created by the false self. But the more you think, the more troubled you feel because thinking, especially negative thinking, takes you farther away from who you really are, not closer. To experience who you really are, you have to drop out of your mind and into your Heart.

Who you really are can be experienced, but it can't be experienced by the mind. The Heart is what is capable of experiencing the truth. It is your link with the Divine as it resides within you. The Divine expresses itself through you, and it uses the Heart to do that, to move you, to inspire you, and to communicate with you. The Heart is where intuition, inspiration, and urges to act arise from. It's not really a place, but it is often experienced as being located in the center of your chest, near the physical heart. It is experienced on a subtle, energetic level, and it communicates energetically, not through words.

Just as the Heart is the point of interface or "control center" of the Divine, the mind is the control center of the *you* that you think of yourself as, or the *ego*. The ego is another name for the false self, or the sense of being an individual, separate from other things and individuals. The ego is the sense of *I*, and it expresses itself mostly in thoughts such as, "I like...." "I am...." "I think...." "I feel...." "I want...." Those are the ego's most common expressions, and such thoughts are nearly always present in the mind. Any thought that begins with "I" is bound to be an expression of the ego because the ego is all about *me*. The sun seems to rise and set around the self that you think of yourself as, or the ego thinks it should!

This makes relationships especially difficult because everyone has an equally self-centered and selfishly motivated ego. It is the fact that we are spiritual beings that allows us to get along with others at all and experience love. Yes, the ego tries to get along with others because getting along increases the likelihood of survival, but without some ability to contact our true nature, relationships would be nearly impossible.

Fortunately, each of us, no matter what our level of spiritual development is, has some contact with who we really are. Our true self, or *Essence*, is felt and does get expressed in many moments throughout our day. We are never far from it. As soon as we turn our attention toward it, there it is. But because Essence isn't experienced by the mind or through the mind, we often miss it or mistake it as nothing because no-thing is closer to the truth of who we are than any *thing*.

Who we really are is not a thing, but more like an experience of no-thingness. Who we are is experienced as emptiness, and when that is experienced, the mind labels it as nothing and turns away from it. This nothingness that we are, however, is what is orchestrating the drama we call our life and every other aspect of life. We are both the creator of our experience and the experiencer. The ego and Essence both have a hand in creating experience, but what experiences is actually Essence. The ego runs from experience by thinking about it or by thinking about the past or the future. When we are identified with the ego, we are experiencing our ideas, not reality.

Who we really are loves experience and is therefore accepting of every experience, and it is possible to feel that acceptance in every moment. However, who we are masquerading as, the ego, is rarely accepting of experience. It opposes life, and that is its role and purpose. If it didn't oppose life, we would experience only the love, acceptance, peace, and joy of Essence. But we are here in these bodies for the time being to experience challenges and overcome them.

Providing challenges is what the ego does. It creates problems by opposing whatever is happening. Whatever is happening becomes a problem the ego needs to fix or something it needs to change or improve upon. Its resistance to life is the biggest challenge of life, and that resistance is the cause of suffering. Essence doesn't have a problem with anything that happens in life. It creates or allows whatever happens. It loves every experience for its own sake and for the growth that comes from it.

The ego and the mind that the ego expresses itself through, which is called the *egoic mind*, provide the grist for our evolutionary mill. The egoic mind, which we experience as a voice in our head and the sense of ourselves as the thinker, is the dragon for the hero to slay, and it is slain with love and acceptance. We are here to learn to love. We are here to overcome fear, hatred, ignorance, and our other negative conditioning with love. Overcoming our negative conditioning brings us Home to Essence, which is where we are intended to go and why it's important to do what we can to heal our conditioning.

Healing our conditioning is also important to our happiness, which depends on contact with Essence. Identification with the egoic mind is a state of unhappiness, discontentment, confusion, fear, and any number of other negative feelings. Happiness is at best fleeting in the egoic state of consciousness. It comes briefly from getting what we want and lasts until the next desire arises. Real happiness comes from being aligned with Essence. True happiness is automatic as soon as we drop out of the egoic mind and into Essence. It doesn't come from getting or having any *thing*, but from just *being*. It is the joy that Essence has in being alive and in being able to experience, because experience is all that Essence requires for happiness—and there's plenty of that.

THE ROLE CONDITIONING PLAYS IN EVOLUTION

Some of our conditioning is necessary and helps us function in the world. Examples of this are certain social rules for behavior. Knowing how to behave in a socially acceptable manner is helpful and smoothes our way in life. Rules that help us function smoothly in society and that help us be safe are examples of positive conditioning. For example, it's a good idea to look both ways before crossing a street, and it's a good idea to avoid eating raw meat. Although these rules aren't always applicable or necessary, following them isn't particularly limiting. Negative conditioning, on the other hand, is limiting and interferes with our ability to function. We could define positive conditioning as anything that doesn't interfere with our functioning or supports it and negative conditioning as anything that interferes with our functioning or with functioning well.

Both positive and negative conditioning serve evolution but in very different ways. Positive conditioning helps us survive and thrive, which is obviously good for our evolution. Negative conditioning, on the other hand, provides the grist for our emotional and spiritual mill. It drives our evolution. Human beings are not intended to be perfect. We are programmed to be fearful and self-centered, and we are programmed with and acquire all sorts of false beliefs that often cause us to react detrimentally and irrationally. These reactions eventually expose our false beliefs because the reactions cause problems, and we learn from the suffering caused by them. We evolve because the suffering caused by our mistaken and negative beliefs causes us to question them. We eventually discover that life goes more smoothly when we hold more positive and true beliefs and when we live from love and unity instead of fear and separation.

Challenges are part of being human, and we are here to overcome them and, in doing so, become stronger, wiser, and more loving. In short, overcoming the difficulties of being human leads to a realization of who we really are and to expressing the qualities of our true nature: love, peace, joy, and acceptance. We are meant to bring these qualities to the world, but first we must overcome the negative programming we were given, which prevents us from feeling love, peace, joy, and acceptance.

Overcoming negative programming is no easy task because we are programmed to not only listen to our thoughts, but also believe them. We believe what we think just because we think it, and we don't generally question what we think. Instead, we question those who disagree with what we think, which is almost everyone else! Everyone is programmed with different beliefs, preferences, desires, and opinions, and everyone believes that theirs are true. It's no wonder relationships are difficult when we are identified with the ego.

There is no hope for seeing things otherwise until we begin to experience who we really are instead of who we are programmed to think we are. To do this, we have to understand that we are programmed to think of ourselves a certain way and that this is an illusion and then we have to desire to experience who we really are. Most of our desires come from the ego, but the desire to know the truth about life and who we really are comes from Essence, and that desire shows up when it is time for us to awaken out of the ego and to begin living from Essence.

THE DIFFERENT TYPES OF CONDITIONING

The different types of conditioning could be categorized as follows:

1. *Conditioning that helps us function in society, be safe, and fulfill our potential.* Examples are rules and beliefs that promote safe, healthy, loving, and otherwise positive behavior. This type of conditioning is considered positive or at least neutral.

2. *Beliefs, prejudices, and opinions we acquire while growing up and continue to acquire from others, our culture and society, and books and other media.* As children, and even as adults, we absorb both verbal and nonverbal messages from our environment. The type of conditioning we absorb this way is mostly negative, since most beliefs and certainly prejudices and opinions aren't true enough to serve us well. Even a belief such as, "women need taking care of," which seems like it could foster caring, is only true in some circumstances. Such beliefs, prejudices, and opinions are generalizations and, as such, have minimal value, and when applied inappropriately, do more damage than good.

3. *Beliefs, prejudices, and opinions we acquire as a result of an experience that we may or may not be consciously aware of.* Much of our conditioning is made up of conclusions we've come to about life and about ourselves and others as a result of our experiences. Some of our beliefs, prejudices, and opinions are the result of conclusions we drew in previous lifetimes, which continue to influence our current lifetime. Like many beliefs, these conclusions often result in a self-fulfilling prophecy. For example, if you concluded you aren't lovable because you didn't get enough love as a child, that belief is likely to cause you to act as if you aren't lovable, and others will take you at your word. That's how beliefs create our reality, or at least our experience of it.

4. *Attitudes, ways of being, behavior patterns, and automatic responses that stem from unconscious beliefs or emotional wounds from this lifetime or others.* Our conditioning is not always conscious. When it is unconscious, it is reflected in our behavior, in certain stances toward life, phobias, compulsions, addictive behaviors, and automatic and sometimes irrational responses. This type of conditioning especially needs healing and is the most difficult to heal because the source is unconscious.

5. *Conditioning/programming that comes from the astrology chart and other esoteric sources.* Our personality and drives are part of our programming, as represented in the astrology chart. Our personality and its drives can be expressed negatively or positively. The programming itself, however, is neither positive nor negative. The character we are playing in this lifetime is unique because it is programmed to be unique. This uniqueness is purposeful and allows the Divine to have a unique experience through us.

6. *Positive, loving beliefs we acquire as a result of our evolution.* As a result of our experiences, we often gain wisdom, or positive conditioning. For example, when as a result of some experience, we conclude that love is more important than things, that is wisdom. The new understanding replaces the ego's erroneous belief that possessions or security are more important than love. Life reconditions or de-conditions the mind by bringing us experiences that can result in wisdom.

All of this conditioning determines our behavior for the most part. Although we have free will and we can act outside our conditioning, we usually don't. Because we are programmed to focus on and believe what we are thinking, our responses and actions generally follow from our conditioning. Until we begin to examine our thoughts and become aware of our conditioning and question it, there is little chance of becoming free of it.

Seeing the truth about your conditioning is the key to getting free of it. Being aware of your conditioning isn't enough if you are still identified with it and believing it. To become free from your conditioning, you have to see the truth about it—that most of it isn't true, helpful, or worth listening to. Once you begin to see how false and unhelpful most of your thoughts are, the spell cast by the egoic mind is broken, or at least greatly weakened, and you can begin to see what else is here living your life.

WHAT KEEPS CONDITIONING IN PLACE

It's usually not necessary to understand where your conditioning came from to become free from it. What's more important is seeing that it is conditioning and not some great truth. We are very convinced of our own beliefs. Even ones that are clearly untrue can be difficult to let go of. This is because we get identity from our beliefs. They give us a sense of being somebody. Who we think we are is exactly that: who we *think* we are! Without your beliefs, you wouldn't be who you think you are. So letting go of even false and detrimental beliefs causes the ego a great deal of discomfort, and it won't welcome this process. Tossing out your beliefs one by one is like tearing the ego apart piece by piece, and it isn't going to go without a fight. And yet all the ego has to fight with is more beliefs—and feelings, particularly fear.

The ego keeps you tied to it and to your conditioning primarily with fear. Giving up certain beliefs feels frightening because you don't know who you'll be without them. Even if they haven't served you well, at least you know who you have been. Not knowing what life will be like without certain beliefs or how you will behave is frightening, so frightening that we often cling to negative beliefs because even they feel better than the unknown.

Exercise: Examining Your Fears

Take a look at your beliefs about yourself ("I am...."). What would happen if you didn't believe those things about yourself? Whether a belief is positive or negative, what are you afraid will happen if you don't believe it? Those fears are what keep that belief in place and keep you tied to that conditioning and certain limiting identities. Even positive beliefs and identities are still conditioning, although positive beliefs are generally preferable to negative ones.

When we are identified with the ego, it seems like our beliefs protect us and keep us safe. We believe we need them to function, so dismissing certain beliefs can feel dangerous. We are afraid that if we stop believing something, our life won't work, we won't be a good person, others will shun us, or any number of other bad things will happen. For example, many believe they are not as good as others. They have difficulty imagining themselves as someone who feels good about themselves. They often feel that if they did picture themselves more positively, they would be pompous, arrogant, or insensitive or unkind to others. They mistake good self-esteem and confidence with arrogance and cruelty. They would rather be the victim than a victimizer, but this is a false dichotomy. Inquiry into your beliefs is likely to reveal many misunderstandings and unfounded fears such as this.

Nearly all of the rules we have about how to live, which can be recognized by the word *should,* are beliefs that feel very threatening to disregard. When you are identified with the ego, it seems that not following these *shoulds* would mean you were a bad person or that you might fail or die. The ego doesn't realize that the goodness that you are sees to it that you behave realistically, practically, and lovingly. The ego feels it must propel you through life with *shoulds.* This simply isn't true.

Essence cares for your existence by guiding you intuitively to do what you need to do to sustain yourself and be happy, and it guides you to do this in a loving and fulfilling way. When the ego takes this on as its job, it carries it out with programmed rules about what and how to do things. The ego would have you work or seek pleasure all the time at the expense of other things, such as love, creativity, and fulfillment. It drives you like a tyrant toward what it wants: success, money, fame, beauty, pleasure, and security. Essence, on the other hand, balances work with play, creativity, just being, and love.

Dismissing the ego's rules and disregarding its drives results in a great deal of fear. What will happen? It feels like you won't survive. The ego keeps you following its dictates with this fear and with other fears: You won't be loved, you won't be happy, you won't be successful.

Exercise: Examining *Shoulds*

Make a list of the shoulds, *or rules, you hold dear: "I should...." Others should...." "Life should...." These are the demands you put on yourself, others, and life, which cause you to suffer. Life is the way it is, but the ego doesn't accept this.* Shoulds *point to a lack of acceptance of the way things are and therefore create suffering. You can have your shoulds or freedom from your conditioning, but you can't have both.* Shoulds *are some of the most difficult conditioning to release because they seem to keep us safe, but do they? And at what cost to our happiness—and other people's happiness?*

Shoulds are not valuable. Feel the resistance the ego has to this statement. It doesn't believe it, and believing it feels scary. The ego has no trust in Essence, in this Intelligence that is living your life, because the ego doesn't believe in Essence. The ego is a self-sustaining concept: Its belief in itself and itself alone sustains it. If the ego believed there was something else here, it could no longer exist, at least not in the same way. As it stands, the ego is dominant in most people's consciousnesses, and the idea of it taking a backseat to something else (Essence) evokes fear and resistance. It's good to notice this fear and resistance. It is the ego's fear and resistance to life, and it is meaningless and untrue. The ego distrusts life, but there is no basis for this distrust.

Life can be trusted because love is behind it all. This is not the point of view of the ego, of course, which is run by fear. The ego would be out of a job if you actually trusted life. Distrust of life is the ego's basic stance, and buying into the ego's distrust keeps you identified with it. The antidote, of course, is trust. However, this is a Catch-22 because the only way to gain trust is to trust. At some point, you have to make the leap of faith, maybe at first by taking baby steps. Eventually, you see that life is supportive and good and that even the challenges it presents are gifts.

To discover the goodness of life, you merely have to look from eyes other than the ego's. The ego sees nearly everything as flawed or bad. Even what it likes, it likes only for a time before judgment sets in and the ego becomes disgruntled with it. You won't find beauty, goodness, or love by looking through the ego's eyes. When you do find these, you are looking through Essence's eyes, which see only beauty, goodness, and love: When the branch moves in the wind, it sees the wind loving the branch and the branch loving the wind. When the sun comes up (or goes down), it sees love in that. When a hummingbird dips its beak into a flower or a raven flies overhead, it sees love in that. Love is all around, when you have eyes for it.

Love is also evident in the fact that we grow from our experiences. We all become better human beings instead of worse ones as a result of life, although some take lifetimes to do that. Life is evolving toward love. In the long run, love always wins out over hatred and negativity. When all of our lifetimes are done, every story has a happy ending.

The ego is myopic; it sees narrowly. It can't see the bigger picture; it can't see where evolution is going. It can't see the wisdom of life or bring you understanding. The egoic mind is not a good guide. We are programmed to trust the mind, but it isn't trustworthy. It tells us not to trust life, but that statement is what we must not trust. Distrust of life is what keeps conditioning in place. To heal, we must find ways to trust in life's goodness.

TRUSTING THAT LIFE IS GOOD

Trusting that life is good isn't easy in light of so much suffering and such inadequate explanations for it. Religions haven't succeeded in explaining this great mystery: Why is there suffering? They've painted a picture of a punitive and vengeful God, a God who behaves toward us as badly as we sometimes do toward each other. Is it any wonder why so many people are angry at God, when they feel that God has caused, or at least allowed, their suffering? Religions fail miserably at explaining life—why we are here and why we experience what we do. How can we trust that life is good when what we are taught to believe about it isn't true?

The misunderstandings and lack of understanding about God are responsible for many people feeling angry at God, and that anger blocks our ability to feel the goodness of life—and to feel Essence. It keeps us tied to the egoic mind, where we aren't able to feel the truth about life and who we really are. Many spend lifetimes caught in this whirlpool of anger and resentment, until one day they find their way clear. Essence breaks through the illusion spun by the ego and the anger, and Essence shows its shining face.

This is the role of spiritual experiences. They are not evidence of any particular level of spiritual development. They are given to us to help us break through to the next level of spiritual understanding or encourage us in that direction. These experiences are often very dramatic and life altering. They are unforgettable, and they change our relationship to life. Often, they catapult us onto the spiritual path, where we continue to seek until we find our way back Home.

Essence doesn't abandon us to the ego, its confusion, anger, and negativity. Essence comes back for us again and again, even as we turn away from it. Many times a day, we turn away from Essence and toward the egoic mind. We don't even notice Essence's peace, love, contentment, joy, and acceptance. The ego doesn't value these because it has other goals. It turns away whenever we touch these qualities of Essence. It isn't interested in them. They leave it with nothing to do, no problem to fix, nothing to judge or complain about or feel superior about. There's no drama in peace, love, contentment, joy, and acceptance, and the ego is all about the drama of the story of *me*.

Essence is so accepting that it even accepts our choice to suffer. It knows that one day we will have had enough suffering and we will come looking for it. It waits patiently for us to notice it and to choose it over the ego. Everyone comes to this point. Everyone eventually chooses Essence over the ego, and that is the happy ending to this story of *me*. The *me* finds happiness and fulfillment by bowing to Essence and kissing its feet. The *me* eventually gets consumed by Essence, and Essence becomes alive in you, as you give it a voice and march to its drummer. Life changes dramatically at the end of our journey here on this plane. It is lived for service to those who haven't found Essence yet, and then we graduate to other planes and realities to serve there as well.

CHAPTER 2

Experiencing Essence

Healing can't occur without an experience of Essence. It is Essence that heals, and it heals in part by bringing us a truer and more complete picture of life and of ourselves. Essence counteracts and neutralizes the negativity of the egoic mind with wisdom, peace, love, joy, and acceptance. But to experience Essence, we have to go against our programming and notice what else is going on in the moment other than thought. When we do that, we drop into the moment, where we experience—and become—Essence.

SEEING RADIANCE

If the Divine had a face, it would be a radiant one. How do we know? Because its reflection on the physical plane is light and radiance and because that's what we see when the Divine, as Essence, looks out from our eyes. The world looks different when we are awake and aligned with Essence. It shines, it glows, it shimmers, it sparkles. People, plants, animals, and objects radiate the light of Being. They always have, but not everyone notices it. The ego doesn't. It's too busy comparing, judging, labeling, and evaluating what it sees to notice the radiance. When Essence looks out of our eyes, however, everything shimmers and shines.

This seeing is not like the usual seeing. It is subtler, but it is still experienced as seeing. It is as if the usual seeing becomes infused with light: The radiance of the Divine spills out of everything. It erases all boundaries and reveals that all is light. All is itself as light. All of creation shimmers as One Being.

Just as the objects in a painting belong to the painting rather than to themselves, the distinctions between objects are no longer seen as real, but as part of the design within a larger whole, which contains them. The painting would not be the same were anything left out. So it is with life: The differences create the Whole; they don't stand apart from it. Furthermore, as in a painting, everything in life is made from the same substance. It is all the Divine.

The mind sees boundaries between the objects in a painting. But by stepping back, the picture as a whole can be experienced, and that is what makes art powerful. Those who love art don't pick it apart and analyze it, but respond to it emotionally and spiritually. So it is with life: The mind picks it apart, and the Heart responds to it spiritually and emotionally (with love).

To see this radiance requires the lenses of perception to be purified, cleansed of the conditioning that perceives boundaries between objects and, moreover, cleansed of the mind's tendency to evaluate what it sees according to its conditioning. Eyes that are directed by the ego look for validation of the ego's viewpoint and threats to its safety and identity. The ego views the world and its contents, including people, from the standpoint of how something will affect its goals: Will it advance my goals or not? The ego is busy with its own inner mental world, not the real world. When it does see the real world, it is through the lens of desire: Will it get me what I want?

The process of healing our conditioning results in a gradual cleansing of the lenses of perception. We gradually come to see more radiance and less according to the ego's desires and goals. This coincides with greater happiness, peace, and contentment with life. The quieter the egoic mind becomes and the less dominant it is, the happier we become. This evolution takes place over many lifetimes. The endpoint is radiance itself: not only do we see radiance everywhere, but we also become radiant.

BEING RADIANT

As the lenses of perception become purified, the gateway to our soul is opened and the Divine begins to shine forth. It does this through the eyes. Once what comes into the eyes is no longer being filtered and distorted by the ego, the eyes become the means by which the Divine receives the world and, in turn, touches it.

The Divine receives the world and everything about the world with acceptance and without judgment. It loves the world. After all, the world is itself, and it has no reason to reject the world. The Divine loves creation for the possibilities it provides for experience. Through creation, the Divine has the opportunity to interact with itself, which as Oneness wasn't possible. What a great adventure and experiment this world is! Not even Oneness knows what its creations, who have lost touch with Oneness to some extent, will do.

This love for the world can be seen in the eyes of those who are in touch with Essence, and it is seen as radiance, love, peace, and joy. Those who see this in someone's eyes are attracted to it because love, peace, and joy are what everyone wants. All the seeking and striving on the part of the ego is an attempt to acquire love, peace, and joy—happiness. The ego just makes the mistake of looking for happiness in the wrong places. In fact, the egoic mind is the only thing in the way of happiness. It is the problem, not the solution. When the mind is quiet, all there is, is love, peace, and joy.

That truth is apparent in the eyes of those who are in touch with Essence. They convey this truth to others through their eyes.

And looking into their eyes can cause others to drop into Essence and experience the same love, peace, contentment, and joy that is the nature of Essence. Wisdom, kindness, and good acts flow from Essence as well. Once the lenses of perception become clear, we become a conduit and catalyst for peace, love, and joy in the world.

The biggest clue to the mystery of who we really are is in the eyes. The Divine gives the secret away by appearing in the eyes. Nowhere else is the Divine more apparent than in the eyes of those who have already discovered the secret: There is only one Being here! When you look into another's eyes, you can feel your commonality with them, your Oneness. You don't have to be enlightened to have that experience, and either does the other person. Oneness shines through in the eyes of everyone.

Eyes can bring you Home if you allow them to. If you allow yourself to drop the thoughts that intervene between you and another for just a moment, then there You are, right there in the other's eyes! What a surprise. We experience this most often during sex and with others we love deeply, such as our children and pets because, with them, our defenses and judgments are diminished. Gazing into another's eyes while affirming your Oneness with them can help bring about the experience of Oneness.

Exercise: Seeing the Divine in Another

Take fifteen minutes or so to sit quietly with someone and look into one another's eyes. Get very comfortable and set aside all issues, concerns, judgments, and any other thoughts to just be present with this person. As you are looking into each other's eyes, just stay with that experience. If a thought comes up, notice it, and then go back to just looking. If your mind wanders, just bring your attention back to the eyes. When the mind isn't being identified with, Essence shines through the eyes. Notice this, without thinking about it or telling any stories about it. Notice the beauty of Essence in your partner. This is his or her true self. This is the Beloved. Beyond conditioning, all there is, is This.

Often, all that is needed to experience Essence is the willingness to. Essence is available in every moment. You just have to notice it and not turn away from it. We are much more willing to do this with people we already love, but it's possible to experience Essence and Essence's love with anyone if you choose to see the truth about him or her.

Even just one person who is doing this in a room full of people can change the atmosphere because Essence is contagious: Essence brings out Essence in others. If you align with Essence, you will become a catalyst for peace, love, and joy in the world. Have you noticed how contagious anger and negativity are? Fortunately, love is equally contagious and a much more rewarding experience.

Practice cultivating loving interactions with others by choosing to see their divine nature, no matter what they are doing or saying or how they look, and you will not only live in peace and joy, but also bring others to peace and joy. Just by noticing the Divine in their eyes, this transformation in you and in others can take place.

Transformation really is this simple, but the ego will come up with all sorts of reasons to discount what it sees in someone's eyes and avoid looking for the Divine there or anywhere else. The ego doesn't believe the Divine exists. It asks: Where is the proof? The ego is afraid of what it sees in the eyes of others. It doesn't know what to think of this. It has no words or explanations for what it sees because that doesn't fit into the ego's paradigm or even into most religious belief systems. The ego doesn't believe there is a Mystery here because the Mystery is not something that can be quantified. All it knows is what it wants, and that becomes the reason for doing and saying what it does.

MOVING FROM THE EGO TO ESSENCE

Everyone experiences Essence several times a day, but the experience is often so brief that it doesn't affect the egoic state of consciousness that most live their lives in. When Essence is experienced for longer periods of time, it can shift us from ego-identification to Essence, which is our natural state. The more we experience Essence, the easier it is to choose it, so we naturally move, over the course of many lifetimes, from ego-identification to Essence because Essence is a much more pleasant state. To live more continually aligned with Essence, the habit of ego-identification needs to be broken, which isn't so easy.

Because we are programmed to pay attention to the egoic mind and believe what it tells us about ourselves, others, and life, most people's lives unfold according to the ego's ideas, desires, and demands—their conditioning. The problem is that happiness can't be found in following the false beliefs and values of the ego. Unhappiness is the certain result of allowing the egoic mind to run your life.

Essence sees life more truly. When we are identified with Essence, we see life more as it really is, without the filter of our conditioning. From Essence, life is interesting, challenging, fun, beautiful, touching, and rich. Experiences aren't categorized, judged, or labeled as good or bad. They just *are*, in all of their richness and complexity, because in truth, a thousand stories could be told about any experience, and those stories would still not reflect the whole experience. The ego attempts to define experience in words, according to its conditioning, which divorces us from the complexity and reality of the experience. It turns experience into ideas, which sap the life out of life. Living from the mind is like eating a picture of food instead of the real thing. No wonder so many people feel empty and unfulfilled. Only reality truly satisfies.

SEEING FROM ESSENCE'S EYES

Seeing from Essence's eyes is a lot like how very young children see. They don't have the degree of conditioning, facts, and concepts yet that older children and adults have, which filter and color experience. The interchange between young children and their environment is much purer. When we are aligned with Essence instead of the ego, conditioning still exists, but it doesn't interfere with experience as it used to. Our thoughts are recognized for what they are: conditioning that is mostly untrue and not helpful.

For the most part, our conditioning takes us down the path to unhappiness, not happiness. So unhappiness and the desire to be truly happy ultimately drive the choice to become aligned with Essence. What stands between us and happiness is essentially just a choice, the choice to be aligned with Essence instead of the ego by saying yes to Essence's perceptions instead of the ego's. Here is an exercise that will help you see from Essence's eyes:

Exercise: Seeing from Essence's Eyes

Look at something in your environment and notice how quickly the mind comes in with a judgment, analysis, or some other comment about what you are looking at. Move your gaze from one object to another and just look and notice what the mind does. As long as you continue to just look without thinking about the object you are looking at, you will see as Essence sees. But the moment you begin to think, you lose contact with the object and with the moment, and you become identified with the ego and its perceptions. Essence doesn't evaluate as it looks; it experiences without evaluation. This looking is joyful and uncomplicated by the negativity of the mind. What a relief it is to be Home! This way of looking can become your ordinary way of seeing and being.

Essence perceives life as a whole and as essentially good. It accepts and loves everything simply because it exists. Essence doesn't demand that life be any way other than the way it is. When you are accepting and loving toward life and your experience, you are experiencing Essence and its love, peace, contentment, joy, and acceptance.

If you stay in acceptance long enough, you will begin to notice the radiance that accompanies the love, peace, and joy you are experiencing. There is a visual accompaniment to being aligned with Essence, which gives objects a shimmery glow and subtle fluidity. Objects are experienced more as flowing into each other rather than having distinct boundaries. The more you pay attention to this subtle visual experience, the longer it lasts and the deeper it becomes. Usually, it's only noticed briefly, but it actually never disappears. Whenever you turn your attention to it, there it is. You can train yourself to see this way more continually, and once your identity shifts more permanently to Essence, that is the experience.

Seeing in this way produces a softness in your eyes and demeanor because Essence's relationship to life is nonviolent and peaceful. Essence takes action when action is called for, but it doesn't try to force or manipulate life to conform to ideas, as the ego does, because Essence is free of ideas about the way things should be. To Essence, the way things are is exactly how they should be.

Essence may have intentions for the next moment, but it doesn't try to change the current one. Essence does influence and shape life, but during it, not after the fact. It flows with life and shapes life while life is moving where it is moving. This is very different from the ego, which opposes whatever is showing up and tries to change what already is.

Those who are strongly identified with the ego often have a hardness and dullness in their eyes, which reflects their determination of will and lack of contact with reality. Nevertheless, Essence shines in those eyes too, behind that hardness and dullness. It flickers in and out, depending on how intensely they are involved with ideas about how things should be. When they are more quiet mentally and relaxed physically, Essence is there in their eyes. Essence is behind everyone's eyes, but it is covered over when mental activity is very strong. You can actually see people thinking.

When you are aligned with Essence, it becomes apparent that Essence is behind your eyes, not only to others, but also to yourself because you feel Essence there. Essence is felt as Consciousness, or Awareness, looking out through your eyes. That Awareness feels like who you are, and your body feels like just a vehicle for moving in the world. Although Awareness isn't limited to the head and eyes, it's often strongly felt in that area because Awareness tends to become localized there.

When you are aligned with Essence, you know yourself as that localized point of Consciousness that is connected to your particular body, mind, and personality. It's clear that the body, mind, and personality are not who you are, but only something that makes it possible for Essence to function in the world. This detachment from the body, mind, and personality makes it possible to see the connectedness and perfection of all of life. It makes it possible to truly love.

When we are aligned with Essence, our eyes have a look to them that is recognizable as Essence but difficult to describe. They have a depth, intensity, and fire about them and a piercing, yet gentle, and infinite quality. An actual energy is transmitted from this gaze, from Essence through the eyes, that can bring others into alignment with Essence to the extent that they are willing to have that experience. This is well known in spiritual circles headed by spiritual masters or gurus. Photos have the same capacity for transmission, even ones of deceased spiritual masters.

In part, this transmission is made possible by the desire and openness of the recipient, who puts himself or herself in a position of receiving by being in the presence of a spiritual master or guru. Doing this is an affirmation of the willingness to experience Essence, and this prayer is always answered, at least to some extent.

The eyes are one of the ways the Divine brings itself Home. They are its calling cards. The eyes indicate the existence of the Divine as well as transmit a frequency that causes those who are ready and open to resonate with their divine nature. The eyes not only provide a visual experience of the Divine, but also have the ability to shift our consciousness.

Those who have experienced the eyes' ability to shift consciousness know the truth on a deep level and need no more convincing, while those who haven't have difficulty believing what they haven't experienced, and understandably so. And yet the Divine is not only experienced through the eyes, but also in many other ways in the world, if only the ego would notice and open to those revelations.

LOVE IS YOUR NATURE

You can tell that love is your nature because love is what you experience when you are still and your mind is quiet. Then the Heart naturally opens, and it expresses itself as love. This love is not romantic love, but more like acceptance, joy, gratitude, and contentment with life. It's subtler, softer, gentler, and less personal than romantic love, which has a giddiness and an excitement about it. With romantic love, we expect the world; with this love, we know ourselves as the world. With romantic love, our focus is on the other; with this love, we know ourselves as the other. With romantic love, there are two; with this love, there is only One.

Our natural state is a state of love, acceptance, peace, contentment, and quietude. Gone is the need to get, keep, improve, and think. In this Stillness, there's little desire for thought or anything else. When you experience love, acceptance, peace, and contentment, it means you have dropped into Essence and are no longer identified with the egoic mind, which can be recognized by the opposite qualities: a lack of love, acceptance, peacefulness, and contentment.

At your core, you are love, acceptance, peace, and contentment. These same qualities are at everyone's core, although they are often obscured by identification with the egoic mind. Ego-identification is the usual state of consciousness, but not the natural state of consciousness. The natural state of consciousness is love, and we are here to discover that. Our programming, which gives us the impression that we are the ego and the mind, conceals this truth.

Love is the glue that holds the universe together. This is an esoteric statement that can't be understood by the mind. We have to take this truth on faith. Once we do, we begin to see love everywhere. Our beliefs have a powerful impact on our experience of life. They filter our perceptions. For example, if you believe that love is everywhere, which it is, then you'll experience that. If, on the other hand, you believe that evil is everywhere, that is what you'll see, no matter how much love is in front of your eyes.

It's important to acknowledge that love is everywhere because doing that counteracts the ego's assumption that love isn't everywhere and that life isn't safe and supportive. The importance of counteracting the ego's negative beliefs is that, unless we do, we are likely to remain identified with the ego. To wake up to our divine nature and live in alignment with that instead of the ego, we have to train ourselves to see life as Essence sees it instead of as the ego sees it. The more we do this, the more Essence will begin to live through us, and we will express Essence in the world instead of the ego. The reward for this is true happiness and peace and the capacity to bring others to true happiness and peace.

EVERY ACT IS AN ACT OF LOVE

Mother Theresa is remembered and revered for her great service to humanity and her ability to see the Divine in everyone. When people think of love and the service that naturally flows from love, she often comes to mind. However, love has many other faces. It is visible in the simplest gestures and acts performed by very ordinary people living very ordinary lives: Love pushes a child on a swing, love drives safely, love shops for food, love listens, love greets, love waves, love touches, love smiles, love laughs, love kisses, love sings, love plays, and loves creates.

Exercise: Noticing Love

Notice all the ways you express love in your life. Notice the ways others express love. Love is everywhere, quietly and simply behind the scenes, being expressed in every moment. The ego's world is absent of love, and when we are identified with it, we see only problems and lack. The ego overlooks the evidence that love is behind and driving all life. Love is the juice that fuels life. We love to move, to breathe, to be alive. We even love to fight and have problems. Essence loves it all, even the chaos, messiness, and chal-

lenges. No matter what is happening, it is possible to experience Essence loving it. Love is really the only constant in the universe.

In fact, everything that people do is an act of love. Even those who choose to steal from or harm others are doing so out of love for themselves because they believe they need to do that to be safe or happy. Not all acts appear loving, but at their core, those who do them have the intention to do good at least for themselves, although possibly at the expense of others.

Harmful acts are attempts, although misguided ones, on the part of those who do them to preserve their own life or get something they feel they need to be happy. As we evolve, we become concerned about preserving the lives of those we love in addition to ourselves. This circle eventually widens to include all of humanity, perhaps even at the expense of our own life.

If we were able to see love in every action, there would be no cause for judgment, which only leads to more separation, hatred, retribution, and suffering in the world. Dropping all judgments doesn't mean we would allow evil and not stand up for justice. Rather, it means we wouldn't be contributing to the separation and hatred that support and feed the sense the ego has that it must oppose others to keep itself safe.

When egos receive love and compassion, they resonate with it and express love, perhaps not immediately if there's a great deal of wounding, but eventually. Love heals, and it helps us evolve out of the fear that is part of ego-identification into the peace of Essence. On the other hand, judgment, hatred, and retribution separate us, which confirms the ego's suspicion that it needs to do everything in its power to protect itself and get what it wants from a hostile world. This negative attitude is contagious, and it creates a very unpleasant world. We can do our part in turning this negativity around by seeing love in every act and remembering that every human being is inherently good.

Affirming someone's inherent goodness allows us to feel compassion for the suffering that person is creating for himself or herself and everyone else involved out of ignorance of the truth. As a result, we become more interested in dispelling ignorance and healing those involved than judging or punishing the wrongdoer. The human condition is such that we are not able to choose well because we don't understand who we really are and what is needed to find true happiness. We make choices that bring suffering to ourselves and others. But this is all part of our spiritual evolution. No one ever became enlightened who wasn't first lost in the illusion of separation and hurting himself or herself and others. Everyone passes through this stage in evolution, and the responsibility falls on those who've already passed this way to help those who lack understanding.

LOVE IS ALL AROUND

As difficult as it may be to see love in certain acts and to see the goodness in certain people, it isn't difficult to find loving acts and loving people in this world. Love shines through in everyone to one degree or another because it can't be hidden or suppressed. Some have discovered the joy of loving acts and practice love consciously. Although most people may not be operating at this level, most do try to be loving to others, especially those close to them. In nearly every interaction, we see people making an effort to be loving. Politeness, smiles, consideration, helpfulness, receptivity, and attention are all ways people show their love and good will. Just because those expressions aren't always pure doesn't diminish the fact that love is driving them.

Although the ego is motivated to get its needs met and most people are identified with it, the Divine is alive and well within everyone and inspiring every person to express love. What interferes with expressing love is the tendency to be absorbed in our mind and thoughts about ourselves and what we want and need rather than about how we might express love.

We can train ourselves to counteract the ego's tendencies. When we decide to dedicate ourselves to expressing love, we choose in each new moment to express love instead of following the egoic mind. Very few people are this committed to love, but that is where spiritual evolution is taking us. It is taking us toward expressing of love in every moment.

ATTENTION

Giving attention is a very basic form of love, which can be seen everywhere, and a way that love can be expressed very simply in the world. What you give your attention to is what you love. If you are giving your attention to the egoic mind, you are loving it and joining with it. If you are giving your attention to others, you are loving them and joining with them. Asking yourself, "What am I giving my attention to?" can be an excellent spiritual practice, and it will help you break the habit of identifying with the egoic mind.

Giving your attention to others is often at odds with giving your attention to your mind because the mind isn't interested in others. It's only interested in itself, its thoughts, its opinions, and its perceptions. To give your attention to others is a gift of love, because to do this, you must override the ego's tendency to give attention to itself and its needs. It takes some effort to overcome the programming to be self-focused and to become more other-focused. When we give our attention to others, we are expressing love in a most basic and simple way.

Giving attention to someone can be a powerful force for good. When you give attention to others, you are channeling love energy to them, regardless of how you might feel about them from the level of your personality. The choice to give attention to others is a loving choice. It connects them with the love energy that is their true nature and yours, and that's a gift. This all happens on very subtle levels, but it's still felt by people, who welcome attention and are often deeply touched by someone paying attention to them. Giving others attention is a way of acknowledging our Oneness with them and catalyzing the experience of Oneness in them, however subtle that experience might be.

Giving others attention causes them to feel love, and that comes back to us and goes out to others as well, so giving our attention to others is ultimately much more rewarding than giving our attention to the mind. Everyone wants love more than anything else because being in touch with our true nature is satisfying, unlike many of the other things the ego tries to attain that bring only fleeting satisfaction. As a result, giving attention to others becomes easier the more it is practiced.

Giving attention is equally rewarding when you give it to whatever you are doing. The ego draws you into its unreal world of thought. It entices you to pay attention to the mind with juicy thoughts about the past, fantasies about the future, and thoughts that build up the ego and sense of being special, which often involve tearing other people down. Giving your attention, instead, to whatever is going on in the moment is an act of loving life rather than rejecting the moment by escaping into the ego's mental world.

Whenever we give our attention to what is actually going on in the present moment, we are rewarded by experiencing love, peace, and contentment. Giving attention to real life instead of to the mind aligns us with love. However, we are programmed to move away from the moment. To counteract thiat programming, you have to learn to give your attention to what is real, to what is showing up *now*. When you do that, you become free of the egoic mind's ceaseless discontentment, negativity, and judgment. All we have ever had to do to be free of suffering is turn our attention away from the mind, away from what is not real, and onto the present moment.

The present moment is where our true nature and the qualities of our true nature can be experienced. Only when we are in the moment fully can we experience real love, acceptance, contentment, peace, and joy. All we have to do to experience those qualities is put our attention on what is happening *now* instead of on our thoughts.

ACCEPTANCE

One of the reasons we turn away from the moment is that we are programmed to reject life as it is. We want life on our own terms, but it can never be that way. Even if the ego could have life on its own terms, which the ego does experience briefly and occasionally, it would soon want more or different or better than that. The ego doesn't accept life, which is one reason the ego doesn't want to give it attention.

The ego would rather give attention to its fantasies, dreams, memories, opinions, judgments, and even fears than to the actual reality of any moment, which in addition to being imperfect (from the ego's point of view), is impossible to control or predict. The unpredictability of life and the ego's lack of control of it are deeply disturbing to the ego. Touching into reality makes the ego very uncomfortable because it is faced with the truth that it's not the one making life happen. As long as the ego remains in its made-up reality, it can play at being king. It pretends that it can make life go its way. It denies the obvious reality and chooses to believe what it wants to about reality.

Accepting whatever is happening drops us into Essence and into a state of happiness, peace, and contentment. That state is immediately uncomfortable for the ego, so the experience of happiness and peace doesn't usually last long. The ego finds fault even with peace, declaring it boring, and drums up a problem to think about and solve. If you agree with the ego's assessment of the moment, you are back in identification with it instead of with Essence. Fortunately, acceptance can bring you right back into the moment. Once you are aware of the power of acceptance to drop you into Essence, you can use acceptance more consciously to do that.

Acceptance is synonymous with love. Love accepts. You could say that acceptance is the definition of love. So when you accept what is happening, you land in love's territory. However, to stay there, you have to keep accepting what's happening, and that can be challenging because the mind comes into nearly every moment with a reason to leave it. You must say no to the mind again and again before its hold is loosened. The more you say no to the mind, the weaker it gets, and the more you say yes to it, the stronger it gets.

Detaching from the mind takes diligence, commitment, and choice, and you are the only one who can make that commitment and choice. To some extent, your spiritual evolution is in your hands. Other factors determine how and when you will unfold spiritually, but how fast you advance is largely up to you and your choices.

Accepting what is happening isn't as difficult as you may think. You only have to accept what is happening in the present moment, not in every moment throughout time. The ego has difficulty accepting what's happening because it spins a negative story about what it means for future moments. For instance, if you are feeling sick, the ego causes you to suffer over it by telling you how awful being sick is and what a negative impact it will have on your life. The stories it spins are all lies. It never predicts the future accurately.

Accepting what's happening is also not as difficult as you may think because accepting it doesn't mean you have to like it. All you have to do is accept that you don't like what's happening, if that is the case. Accepting what's happening just means you are willing to let it be the way it is. After all, what other choice do you have, since it is the way it is?

The only other choice is to argue with what's happening, complain about it, try to ignore it, or try to change it, which is what the ego does in nearly every moment. This is a recipe for suffering and doesn't change what is happening; it only makes what's happening unpleasant. By allowing whatever is happening to be happening, you align yourself with life instead of opposing it, and that makes every moment, regardless of what is happening, peaceful.

When the moment is okay just the way it is and your energy is not taken up in opposing it, you can really be present to whatever is happening. What you discover is that every moment has much more to it than what you like or don't like about it. Every moment is rich with complexity, dimension, and beauty. The ego paints the moment as black or white, good or bad. It has a simplistic view of what is happening according to its likes and dislikes, but the moment is not simple in the least. It's interestingly changeable, unpredictable, and intelligent. Who knows what will happen next? You never know. From the perspective of Essence, life's unpredictability is delicious, exciting, and fascinating. When you are in acceptance, you feel that way too about life.

When you are accepting, you are expressing Essence. And when you are accepted by others, you are experiencing Essence. Think of all the times in one day you are either accepting or experiencing acceptance from others. Every time acceptance happens, Essence is showing up in your life. Love is everywhere in the form of acceptance: You accept the sky, you accept gravity, you accept your breathing, you accept the color of the trees, you accept the silence between sounds, you accept the space between objects. You accept the majority of what is. This is You loving life and allowing it to be the way that it is.

The mind interrupts this peace, this love, by telling you that something is not right, not good, not desirable: "That dog shouldn't be barking." "The sun shouldn't be so hot." "It shouldn't be so windy." If you agree with the mind, you suffer. If you don't, you stay in Essence, in allowing whatever is to be the way it is.

The egoic mind will tell you that accepting life means you won't ever do anything. It tries to scare you out of accepting by making acceptance equal to passivity, laziness, and a lack of discrimination, which the ego deems dangerous to survival. Acceptance is dangerous to the ego's survival, but it's not dangerous to your survival. Acceptance is a more effective strategy for survival than anything the ego has to offer. Acceptance is love, and love connects us with everything because it connects us with who we really are, which is everything. What could be more beneficial to survival than being connected to everything and knowing you are everything? Is there any reason that You, as the Divine, would not take care of you, as the creation? You are being taken care of and so is everyone else.

The ego not only can't take credit for your survival, but it has interfered with it more than it has helped.

Something else besides the ego is living your life, and the more you allow it to do that, the more it will take over. Essence has been living through you and expressing itself through you as much as you have allowed it to. Every person is an expression of Essence to a greater or lesser degree. The Divine is moving, speaking, doing, creating, laughing, playing, and working through each of us to the extent that we allow it to, but it is there in everyone. If you want to have an experience of the Divine, you are having it! And so is everyone else.

You are not separate from the Divine. The ego is the sense that you are a separate person apart from the Divine, but that is just an idea. The ego is just the idea, "I exist as a separate entity." It isn't true. You are the Divine in disguise as a human being. The more you come to see that you are not who you think you are, the more you will experience who you really are and who everyone else really is. The Divine is everywhere.

CHAPTER 3

Healing Conditioning with Positive Thoughts

TRUSTING THE HEART

It may seem strange to heal conditioning, which is thoughts, with more thoughts, but reprogramming the mind with positive thoughts can help us become free of negative or false conditioning and free of identification with the egoic mind. A negative mind, which is how the mind is programmed to be, is difficult to detach and disidentify from. Negativity is compelling. The fear that is associated with a negative mind binds you to it. It captures your attention like nothing else and makes it difficult to give your attention to anything else.

Fear not only can be paralyzing, but it can also drive us in directions that aren't fulfilling. Trying to avoid what the ego fears can take up a lot of energy and cause us to put our energy into unfulfilling and unsuitable activities. For instance, many people work at jobs they dislike and aren't suited for instead of risking doing what they love because they are afraid of not being able to support themselves. They don't realize that Essence has intentions for us that, when followed, bring us happiness and fulfillment. The form Essence's intentions take may not be what the ego had in mind, but it will, nevertheless, feel right and good.

Happiness is possible for everyone, but you won't find it by taking your mind's advice. The egoic mind is very quick to advise us about life, but it doesn't know what we're best suited for or what will make us happy and fulfilled. To discover this, we have to listen to our Heart. If we don't trust our Heart, we'll end up listening to our mind instead. Before we can let go of the beliefs that keep us tied to the egoic state of consciousness, we have to learn to trust our Heart to some degree. That trust develops gradually over time, even over lifetimes. We evolve from not being in touch with our Heart and not trusting it to trusting it completely.

The only way to develop trust is by trying it out. You see what happens if you trust your Heart, first in little ways and then in bigger ways. You eventually learn how to tell what the Heart is saying by following what you think it's saying. You get increasingly better at understanding how it communicates and at following through on those messages.

The ego interferes with following your Heart through doubts, judgments, confusion, worry, and fear. It jumps in with questions, comments, facts, and other statements that cause you to question the Heart's communication. Or once you've received the Heart's message, it tries to take over the process of following it. Many know what the Heart wants, but they follow the ego's suggestions about how to get that, which may take them in a direction the Heart might not have. The less aware you are of the ego's voice and tactics, the more likely you are to be sidetracked by it.

How to Differentiate Between the Ego's Voice and the Heart

It isn't difficult to tell the difference between the ego's voice and the Heart's. The ego's voice comes in the form of thoughts, and the Heart's rarely does. The Heart's communication comes in the form of intuition, which may later get cloaked in words, and in the form of urges, drives, and inspiration that spur action spontaneously.

The most obvious difference is that the ego's voice is negative and uses negative emotions, such as fear, guilt, shame, and anger to spur us to action, while the Heart's voice is one of encouragement, love, kindness, gentleness, support, and acceptance. It uses positive emotions, such as joy, happiness, elation, peace, and love, to spur us on.

Why do we even listen to the negative voice of the ego when the Heart's voice is so loving? The answer is simply that we are programmed to listen to the egoic mind and to overlook the Heart's communications. Because the Heart speaks in the subtle language of energy, not words, a certain amount of spiritual development is necessary to hear it or be willing to hear it. There comes a time in our evolution when we are ready to be done with the suffering caused by listening to the egoic mind and ready to listen to something else. Before that, we are willing to have the ego structure our life with its desires, fears, beliefs, ideas, feelings, and drives. This is fine with the Divine, which welcomes the experience, learning, and growth that result from following the mind. The Divine is interested in having the human experience, or it wouldn't have created us to be the way we are. But after a time, we are meant to wake up out of the false self and discover who we really are.

IDENTIFYING NEGATIVE BELIEFS

Negative thoughts belong to the ego. Positive thoughts, on the other hand, often represent positive conclusions we've come to as a result of our evolution, and they come from Essence. You could say that Essence is teaching us love through every experience we have. It makes us wise by encouraging us to draw positive, loving conclusions from our experiences instead of negative ones. These positive conclusions become part of our programming, which we can draw on and apply to other experiences. These positive conclusions replace certain negative programming, and that's how evolution proceeds: As we evolve, we become more positive and loving and less negative and fearful. We grow toward love, and so does our mind. It becomes more positive as we evolve.

This is generally a slow and sometimes painful process, as our lessons don't necessarily come easily. We learn to love and accept primarily by being given no other option but suffering. When life becomes very difficult, we have two choices: to accept what is happening or to resist it and suffer. When we discover that love and acceptance are the way out of suffering, we begin living more in love and acceptance and less in the ego's fear and negativity. Fortunately, we can speed this process along by purposefully discovering positive ways of looking at things. When we replace a negative belief with a positive one, it erases the negative belief, and the positive one becomes the basis for our automatic responses to life instead of the negative one.

We can become skillful at recognizing the negative beliefs that keep us from happiness and spiritual freedom and replacing them with positive ones. The process is quite simple, but not necessarily easy to apply because of the diligence and commitment required to reprogram the mind. The first step in reprogramming the mind is to notice a belief that is detrimental to you. How do you know it's detrimental? When you believe it, you feel contracted (tight and tense energetically and physically), fearful, angry, bad about yourself, bad about others, or bad about life. Those are signs that a belief is part of the ego's programming.

Many beliefs cause problems for us and cause us to feel contracted, but the most detrimental (and untrue) ones come charged with negative feelings. Anger, sadness, regret, guilt, resentment, shame, and other negative feelings are sure signs that you are identified strongly with a belief that has very little truth to it. The more false or negative a belief is, the more contracted it makes us feel. "Negative" could be defined as not having much truth because, at its core, this is a positive universe. For instance, is it true that no one loves you? You may feel that it's true, but it's a very untrue belief. It may be your experience on a feeling level, but love is abundant in the universe if you are open to receiving it. Anyone who is not feeling loved is not allowing themselves to feel the love that is present.

It is also true that this positive universe is full of challenges. The ego defines challenges as bad, but Essence doesn't. Every experience is what you tell yourself about it. You can spin a negative story or a positive one, depending on how you look at an experience. Essence sees the positive, and the ego sees the negative. We are here to learn to see the beauty in every experience, as Essence does. The alternative is to suffer. Suffering is used in this dimension to catalyze a different viewpoint and point us toward love. It isn't this way in every dimension, but that's how it is in this one. Not accepting that only creates more suffering.

After identifying a negative belief you'd like to change, you need to examine it for other related beliefs that keep it in place because those will also have to be addressed. Mistaken beliefs tend to generate others. A belief is usually part of a complex of beliefs, which will have to be seen and neutralized with various positive statements. For example, it's common for those who were abused as children to believe they are unlovable. Children take their experience personally and blame themselves for it. They might also conclude any number of things as a result of abuse: "I'm not good enough." "I'm not smart." "I don't deserve to be happy." "I will never be happy." "I'm bad." "I'm powerless." "Men are cruel." "Life is cruel." "I don't want to be alive." The list goes on. If negative beliefs didn't tend to generate other negative beliefs, they would be much easier to overcome.

Feelings also make reprogramming negative beliefs a challenge. When a belief has strong feelings attached to it, that belief feels very true. Feelings make beliefs especially believable. Feelings feel much more real than thoughts. Feelings cause physical reactions in the body and motivate actions. They are, in fact, the fuel that translates thought into action. Beliefs that have strong feelings tied to them don't stay in the realm of thought, but spill out into reality through action. Beliefs fueled by feelings often cause people to harm themselves and others. Because negative feelings are uncomfortable, people often try to get rid of them by taking action. The problem with doing this is that it doesn't address the real cause of those feelings, which is mistaken beliefs.

Our strong feelings indicate the mistaken beliefs that most need to be seen and replaced with positive ones; however, these detrimental beliefs aren't always obvious, and some are unconscious. To discover the beliefs behind a negative feeling, we have to be willing to be with that feeling without repressing it or expressing it. This takes awareness, will, and commitment to uncovering the truth and freeing ourselves from those beliefs. However, when we feel bad, we are inclined to react automatically and often lack the will to do otherwise. Commitment to becoming free from conditioning requires summoning some will and commitment where there generally is none. The path of least resistance is to express or act out our feelings, and many people are convinced that that is the proper way to deal with feelings.

Psychotherapy encourages people to express their feelings, and doing that is better than repressing them because at least there is awareness of them, and repressed feelings aren't driving behavior unconsciously. Psychotherapy encourages people to express their feelings positively and constructively, and that is to its credit. However, doing that doesn't free people from their conditioned reactions; it only makes their conditioned reactions more socially acceptable. That advice is appropriate for a certain stage in our evolution, but to become free from conditioning, something else is required: learning to be with your feelings without expressing them or repressing them. Here is how to do that:

Exercise: Being with Your Feelings to Uncover Mistaken Beliefs

When you are experiencing a feeling, just allow it to be there without either feeding it with more thoughts or pushing it aside. Bring to whatever you are feeling the same curiosity and acceptance that a parent would bring to a hurt child to try to uncover the child's pain. You wouldn't bully a child to find out what is going on, and approaching feelings that way doesn't help either. Instead, you act toward your feelings as Essence would act, and doing that allows the feelings to be seen and released. Love, gentleness, kindness, acceptance, and a nonjudgmental attitude are what is needed to release feelings and uncover mistaken beliefs.

Being with a feeling in this way allows you to uncover the beliefs that gave rise to it. What were you thinking that caused you to feel that way? Is it true? What else were you thinking? Is it true? Keep looking for beliefs that are connected to that feeling and keep asking, "Is it true?" None of your beliefs are ultimately true.

Feelings happen as a result of what you say to yourself, either consciously or unconsciously. By staying with a feeling with an attitude of curiosity and acceptance, the complex of beliefs that triggered the feeling can be uncovered.

This process can take some time, and it may need to be repeated many times before the beliefs and feelings begin to let go. Those beliefs have been there for a very long time, so we can't expect them to disappear the instant we first see them, but seeing them repeatedly in this way, with compassion and acceptance, eventually allows them to release their hold on us. You bring Essence to them, not the ego, and Essence does the healing.

You don't need to understand or even believe in this process for it to work. You just have to give it a chance, and you will see for yourself that it does work. There is great healing power in acceptance. That is clear from psychotherapy. That love and acceptance can free us from our suffering is also proof that love is the guiding force behind all life.

When you sit with a feeling, you invite it to reveal the reasons it is there, and you wait patiently for the answers. This is a time of receptivity, which requires that you not be involved in thinking. Thoughts may come and go, but the insight won't come in the form of thoughts. What you are waiting and listening for is an intuitive knowing to arise. Intuitions are automatically put into words once they do arise, but the process is not one of thinking about possible beliefs or trying to figure them out. Instead, your mind is quiet so that you can "hear" your intuition tell you the belief behind the feeling, and you wait for as long as it takes.

Sitting quietly and waiting affirms your commitment to healing and makes it more possible for your intuition to be heard. The desire to understand the beliefs that produced the feelings and the willingness to take the time to listen opens you up to receiving answers. To get answers from Essence, that is really all that is ever necessary, just a willingness to ask for help and receive it.

When you are doing this investigation, expect that there will be a number of beliefs behind any feeling, and don't just settle for one. Keep listening. Uncovering these beliefs is similar to peeling away the layers of an onion: Uncovering one belief allows you to see the next one. Allow the discovery process to continue as long as it needs to until you feel a sense of completion. Then be willing to do it again if the same feelings arise around a similar circumstance. Doing this will greatly weaken the conditioning and its ability to cause you to react automatically and unconsciously.

Some beliefs that drive our behavior negatively are unconscious. This is especially true of addictions and compulsions. Being with a feeling in the way that was just described can even uncover unconscious beliefs. Bringing awareness to your feelings without acting on them allows unconscious beliefs to come to the surface. By accepting your feelings and listening to them, you create a safe environment for unconscious material to arise, and so it will. This is why unconscious material often surfaces during meditation. You invite healing by relating to your thoughts and feelings in this gentle, accepting way. Being with feelings this way can greatly speed up your evolution and ease your way through life.

When you work with feelings in this way, you may also receive a mental picture or simply a knowing about an event in the past that was responsible for the negative conclusions you came to. These images may be repressed memories from this lifetime or from another. These images can be helpful in understanding why you came to the conclusions you did, but you don't need to know the details of the event. It is more helpful to experience the person you were then and to give that person compassion, acceptance, and forgiveness, if necessary. You bring Essence's love, acceptance, wisdom, and compassion to the confused person that came to confused conclusions in the midst of a traumatic event. And you offer the same to anyone else who was involved in the traumatic event. This love and acceptance is what heals, more than uncovering the specific details of what happened. It's much more important to understand what you concluded as a result of some event than to understand exactly what happened or even who was involved.

REPLACING NEGATIVE BELIEFS WITH POSITIVE ONES

Once you've uncovered each belief, it's helpful to find a statement that will counteract or neutralize it. The best statement isn't always the opposite of the belief or the negation of it. Sometimes, the opposite belief (e.g., "I'm lovable" instead of "I'm not lovable") is too big a leap for the unconscious mind and therefore unbelievable. Other statements may work better. For example, if the belief is "I'm not lovable," any of the following statements might be effective in neutralizing it because the unconscious mind might see them as believable: "I am loved by God." "I am open to receiving love." "I freely and gladly give love." "I am a child of God." "Love is here now." "Love is always available." "Love fills me and flows through me." "Love is abundant." "Love is everywhere."

Affirming the presence and abundance of love and your willingness to receive it opens you up to love, while "I'm not lovable" closes you off to the love that is available to you. These affirmations about love are the truth, and the truth will set you free, as they say. Affirming Essence's truth instead of the ego's aligns you with Essence and heals whatever is false within you. Healing conditioning is really just a matter of moving from the ego's false perspective to Essence's, and you do that by affirming Essence's perspective instead of the ego's.

The key, then, is to find what Essence would say to you instead of your ego. Believing Essence's perspective instead of the ego's frees you from your conditioning. By neutralizing the complex of beliefs behind your feelings, the feelings diminish and eventually

Healing Conditioning with Positive Thought 53

disappear, and then it's easy to see that your conditioning is just thoughts that arise in your mind and then disappear. Without feelings attached to them, the thoughts don't have as much power to catch you up. They seem less real, less true, and less compelling. Reprogramming your mind with positive thoughts diminishes the power of the negative thoughts, as the positive ones become stronger. Eventually, the negative thoughts will no longer arise, and the positive thoughts will be your natural state. Here is an exercise that will help you reprogram your negative beliefs:

Exercise: Reprogramming Negative Beliefs

Make a list of negative beliefs you hold about yourself, life, and others. For each belief, counteract it with a positive statement or statements—something Essence would say about you, life, or others. Be your own wise healer by responding to your negative beliefs with the kindness, compassion, and wisdom of Essence. Doing this will help neutralize the negative belief and any feelings attached to it. Repeat this exercise whenever a negative beliefs arises, especially when there are feelings attached to it.

This process does take time, especially if the conditioning is very strong and laden with feelings and if there are many beliefs attached to it. So you take one belief at a time, and when that belief is seen through, you notice what other beliefs remain. What other belief or beliefs are holding the feelings and the behavior related to those feelings in place? Work on whatever beliefs you are aware of, and eventually the issue will clear. How long it takes to clear an issue depends on a number of things and isn't entirely up to you, so be patient. It can take as long as a few years for some issues to clear. Meanwhile, they will become increasingly less of a problem. It's important to acknowledge your progress so that you continue with this work and don't become discouraged. There's nothing to lose and everything to gain. You'll find that it's well worth it.

One thing that can undermine our determination to heal an issue is the belief that it's too difficult to heal. This belief comes from the ego, of course. The ego will try to discourage you with doubts and negative remarks: "Why bother?" "It won't make a difference." "You just have to live with it." "You just have to accept being this way." "It's just the way you are." These remarks may seem harmless enough. They are the kinds of things we say to ourselves all the time, but they can subtly undermine our will and determination to be free. These kinds of statements belong to the ego. It doesn't want you to be free of your conditioning because it would be out of a job.

The ego also uses fear to keep us from being free from our conditioning: "If you stop thinking you're fat, you'll probably let yourself go." "If you don't keep the house spotless, people will judge you." "If you were really happy, you probably wouldn't accomplish anything." Be sure to be aware of such beliefs because the fear of those consequences is likely to be what keeps you from being free. Here is an exercise that will help you uncover the fears that keep your negative beliefs in place:

Exercise: Uncovering Fears that Keep Beliefs in Place

Some beliefs are held in place by fear. To release these beliefs, ask yourself, "What am I afraid will happen if I don't believe that?" Find the fears—all of them—see the falseness of those fears, and then counteract those beliefs with positive statements.

For example, take the belief "I will never be happy." What if you didn't believe that? One answer might be that you would try to be happy and you might fail. Having the belief that you will never be happy keeps you from having to try to be happy or having to discover what makes you happy and from the disappointment you might experience if you failed. The belief, itself, blocks your happiness because why would you even try to be happy if you believed you could never be happy? Then being an unhappy person becomes part of your identity. Who would you be if you weren't an unhappy person? Sometimes it feels better to have any identity, even one as an unhappy person, than an uncertain one. Once an idea becomes part of our identity, we become attached to seeing ourselves that way and we even do things to prove it to ourselves and others.

Conditioning that relates to the self-image ("I am....") keeps you tied to a certain way of thinking about yourself, which becomes comfortable because it's familiar, even if it isn't a positive way of thinking about yourself and even if it isn't very true. If you were told to think of yourself a certain way by your parents, proving them wrong might seem wrong to you. Children take on identities that others give them, even when those identities are harmful or don't fit, until they have the courage to see things differently.

Your self-image is just that, an image, an idea, nothing more. It has no power to shape you except the power you give it. If you think of yourself a certain way, your actions and words follow suit, and pretty soon others agree with your self-image. Negative self-images, and even some positive ones, are limiting because they represent only a sliver of the truth, although when you believe them, they often become more true. To exchange a negative self-image for a truer one, you only need to see how limited and false the old image is and start believing you are divine, loving, and good (and other qualities of Essence).

How do you start believing something when you don't believe it? You just decide to believe it, and you reinforce your belief in it with self-talk and images that represent it, and you don't give your attention to thoughts and images that don't represent it. What you focus on, you become. The mind creates your internal reality. If you have a positive mind, you have a positive internal reality; if you have a negative mind, you have a negative internal reality. A positive internal reality is attractive when expressed, and a negative internal reality isn't. Positive thoughts attract, while negative thoughts repel. That's why it seems like we create our reality with our thoughts. Life does deliver more good things to those who have positive minds than to those who don't. This doesn't mean, however, that you can get anything you want by imagining it or declaring it. That's quite a leap from the previous statements.

Let's take another example. The belief that you are a failure and that you will never be successful may be the result of a self-image your parents gave you or it may be a conclusion you came to because of some failure. Many other beliefs may be attached to it, such as: "I'm not as smart as others." "I don't have what it takes." "I don't fit in." "I don't like to work." "I need to be taken care of." "I can't handle responsibility." There also may be fears that keep the belief that you are a failure in place: fear of failure, fear of being someone who is successful, fear of being unloved, fear of responsibility, and on and on. The conclusion that you are a failure, like many other conditioned beliefs, becomes part of your self-image. You see yourself a certain way, and you may even picture yourself a certain way physically as a result of this belief.

This complex of beliefs would also cause you to have any number of feelings: You may feel sad, angry, ashamed, fearful, or jealous. These feelings don't stay hidden very well, especially when circumstances trigger this conditioning. These feelings can interfere with relating to others, particularly with coworkers and employers. The belief that you will never be successful also affects your body posture and actions: You act insecure, self-conscious, and unconfident, and others see this and believe what you believe about yourself. This belief, then, becomes a self-fulfilling prophecy.

What is the solution? First you have to become aware that you are creating the experience of being unsuccessful *in part* by your beliefs. However, it seems important to add that you aren't creating everything in your life by your beliefs, and changing your beliefs isn't going to make your life become exactly as you would like it to be. That is magical thinking. Changing your beliefs will only open up possibilities that your negative beliefs blocked.

By the way, is there really anything such as failure or success? Success and failure are concepts created by the ego and have no intrinsic reality. These concepts are judgments on the part of the ego, and the ego creates a self-image based on these judgments. From the point of view of Essence, mistakes (what the ego calls failure), lead to learning, and learning leads to not making that mistake again. And that's progress, which can ultimately lead to what the ego experiences as success. That's the truth about life, but the ego will spin a negative tale whenever it can.

Once you are aware that you are creating the experience of feeling unsuccessful, both by how you think about your experiences and by the self-image you project, you can begin to deconstruct that self-image and replace it with a more positive and true one. That new self-image might include "I'm someone who has grown from my mistakes" or "I'm someone who is willing to make an effort and learn" or "I have as much right to success as anyone." Here is an exercise that will help you transform your negative self-images:

Exercise: Transforming Your Self-Images

Take whatever negative story you have spun about yourself and spin it differently—more positively. Try to see yourself and your experience as Essence or a loving parent would. What would Essence say to encourage you to trust life and trust yourself and open up to new possibilities? Examine what you've said to yourself about yourself and your life, weed out the negative statements, and find new, more positive ways of speaking about yourself and about life. Whatever leads to feeling at peace, loved, and supported is a truer statement than anything that leaves you feeling contracted, fearful, powerless, angry, or ashamed.

Next, if there are negative emotions that accompany your story about yourself, allow yourself to just be with them, one at a time, to discover the mistaken conclusions you came to that caused those feelings. Take your time doing this because it is a very important step. It's very difficult to change your conditioning when feelings keep getting triggered. You will know you are succeeding when the negative feelings lessen and aren't triggered as often. To uncover any fears around letting go of your beliefs, ask, "What am I afraid will happen if I don't believe that?" and see what other beliefs keep that negative self-image in place.

HEALING CONDITIONING IN RELATIONSHIPS

These same principles can be applied when your conditioning gets triggered in relationships. First of all, it's important to realize that your preferences, opinions, judgments, beliefs, and reactions to others are all part of your conditioning. As such, you are responsible for them in the sense that no one else caused them, although others do trigger them. Nevertheless, you didn't ask for that conditioning. For the most part, it was just given to you. You could say you inherited it, from your family, experiences, culture, previous lifetimes, and astrology chart. It's your particular programming for this lifetime, and it is no better or worse than anyone else's conditioning, which they also inherited.

The problem is we assume that our conditioning is right and other people's (when it's different) is wrong. This unconscious assumption is what causes problems in relationships, not the conditioning itself. If we can allow others to be different from us, then conditioning doesn't have to be a problem. But we tend to judge others who do and see things differently than we do and try to change them. Our conditioning is bound to be different from someone else's; we're designed that way. So having different conditioning (i.e. beliefs, preferences, opinions, styles, ways of being) doesn't have to be a problem unless we make it one.

We tend to hold our conditioning as inviolate: We want what we want, we like what we like, we don't like what we don't like, and we believe what we believe. Our conditioning feels important, meaningful, and worth fighting for. That's where we get into trouble. Conditioning is just beliefs, preferences, and desires (which are just the thought "I want" with feelings attached to it). Conditioning comes from the ego, not from Essence. While the ego will fight with others over what it believes, likes, and wants, Essence chooses love over beliefs, preferences, and desires. If you want relationships to work, that's what you have to do as well. If even just one person in a relationship is willing to choose love over what he or she believes, prefers, or desires, a loving relationship is possible. If not, then the relationship will be a battleground over conditioning.

When your conditioning gets triggered in relationship, it's an opportunity to discover more about that conditioning. Feelings are a sign that your conditioning has been triggered: You feel angry or sad or some other negative emotion in relation to the other person. When that happens, the tendency is to say, "You make me angry when..." or "You make me sad when...." We think it's good mental hygiene to let others know how they are affecting us. We were taught to do this, but it isn't actually helpful. It puts the burden of change on the other person, when it really lies with us.

If you feel angry or sad over something someone said or did, that's a sign that your conditioning is interfering with love. When feelings like these arise, there is a choice to be made between your conditioning or love: Is your conditioning more important than love, or is love more important than your conditioning? Most people fight for their conditioning because it feels like their conditioning is who they are: "I'm someone who believes..." or "I'm someone who likes...." Their identity is tied to their conditioned beliefs, and without their beliefs, it feels like they wouldn't be who they are. And they wouldn't be. They wouldn't be who they *think* they are; they would be who they really are: Essence.

Most people also deeply believe that they can change others and that it's their duty to do so because they believe their conditioning is superior. They choose trying to change others to fit their own conditioning over loving them. This choice leads to misery in relationships. No one wins the battle of conditioning. Everyone loses love. Even if you get the other person to change, at what expense is that accomplished? And at what point do you finally give up trying to mold the other person to your conditioning? The ego is never satisfied, and it always finds more improvements to push for in relationship, as in every other aspect of life.

Relationships are meant to be a safe haven in the storm of life. They are our best chance for finding love and acceptance. They also serve as a laboratory for love: They are where we learn about love. What we learn is that only Essence knows how to love, not the ego. To create that safe haven, you have to move out of the ego and drop into Essence, where love is possible. Our desire for love and relationship motivates us to overcome our conditioning and live in Essence more because that's the only way it's possible to feel love and maintain it. We learn this by first trying to get our way in relationships and then finally surrendering to love. The secret of many couples who stay together for decades is that they accept each other. Each allows the other to be the way he or she is.

You might argue that acceptance enables your partner to continue his or her bad habits, when who could help him or her better than you? What is true in the realm of personal healing is also true in interpersonal healing: Acceptance is what heals. That is Essence's way. Acceptance is not the ego's way, but the ego isn't trying to help others as much as it's trying to get its way. If you really want to help someone, then accept that person and just see what miracles love and acceptance can perform. Here is an exercise for healing your relationships:

Exercise: Healing Relationships

Your job in relationships is not to change others, but to release any ideas that keep you from being loving and accepting. To do that, notice when feelings are triggered, and then give curiosity, acceptance, and attention to those feelings until you discover what beliefs are behind them. Then examine how true each of those beliefs are. You will find that none of your beliefs are true, at least not true enough to warrant withholding love from another. All of your beliefs are just conditioning.

Let's take an example: Your husband eats with his mouth open and has other bad table manners. When you notice this, you feel judgmental and ask him to change his behavior. When he doesn't, you feel anger on top of judgment. Judgment is always a sign of conditioning. Judging is one of the ego's favorite activities because finding fault with others makes it feel superior. Judging is also a way we attempt to change others, but it doesn't work, and we don't seem to see that it doesn't work. "It should work!" says the ego. So when it doesn't, we feel angry.

Anger is an opportunity to examine our conditioning. In this instance, you might find that your self-image is that of someone who is "higher class," and bad table manners contradict this self-image. You were brought up in a family that emphasized good table manners and punished you for not conforming, so table manners seem very important, perhaps even a matter of life or death (from the standpoint of a child). What will happen if you let go of judging your husband and allow him to eat however he eats? You discover that you are afraid that others will judge you, that they will look down on you harshly and reject you (as your parents did) and perceive you as lower class, which was your parents' fear.

Seeing this, you allow those feelings of judgment, anger, and fear to be there and continue to glean what you can from them. Based on your experience as a child, these feelings are perfectly reasonable. Of course, you would feel that way. But now, as an adult, you can see that this reaction is out of proportion to the circumstances. Is it true that people will judge you and your husband and reject you for his table manners? It's true that some people might judge him because that's what egos do, and most people are identified with their egos. Some might even reject you. Would that be so bad? When you are a child, a parent's rejection can threaten your survival, but would rejection in this circumstance threaten your survival? No, of course not. Seeing this will diminish the emotion attached to this complex of beliefs.

After seeing this, you realize there are still some other judgments and reactions associated with the way your husband eats. He doesn't fit your idea of how your prince charming should behave, so you feel rejecting of him. "He eats like a child," you say to yourself. "I want a man, not a child." Thoughts like these are how the ego undermines love. The ego finds reasons not to love, and it feels justified in its point of view. Although there is some truth to these thoughts, does eating like this mean your husband is a child? The statement "He eats like a child" implies that he is a child, but of course, that isn't true. And how important is it, really, that you get what you want? Must life conform to your preferences and desires? Is that the measure of happiness? One way the ego creates unhappiness is by comparing how life is right now with some unattainable ideal or at least some idea that isn't true right now. Is your idea or ideal more important than loving this man right now? You have a choice. You can choose your conditioning or love, but you can't have both. What will it be?

WHEN POSITIVE BELIEFS ARE NOT HELPFUL

Positive beliefs that come from Essence are true and helpful in counteracting negative conditioning. Beliefs that come from Essence are wise and loving aphorisms, such as: "Love is what matters." "All is well." "Inner beauty is more important than outer beauty." "There's no such thing as failure." "You'll never know until you try." "Life is always changing." "You never know." "There's enough love to go around."

However, positive beliefs can also come from the ego, in which case, they may not be any truer than negative ones. The ego believes a lot of positive things that aren't true. For instance, it might believe you will win the lottery or be famous or that you are the best violinist on earth. Although you might win the lottery or be famous or be the best violinist on earth, these beliefs are much more likely to be false than true. The ego pumps itself up with grandiose imaginations and fantasies. One of the ways it copes with life is to pretend to be something it's not. Beliefs that support such illusions and lack of realism do much more harm than good. They are examples of self-delusion, not positive thinking.

What allows such unrealistic beliefs to proliferate is the belief that believing something can make it so. Everyone has had experiences where this has happened: You believed something would happen, and it did. The fact that sometimes what you believe happens causes some people to conclude that believing is what made it happen. This is magical thinking. Believing that you will win the lottery, for instance, obviously doesn't cause you to win it, or many more people would be winners. Besides, a lot of things happen to people that they didn't believe would happen.

What often does happen, though, is that people have an intuition of something that's going to happen, they believe that intuition, then when it happens, they conclude that their belief made it happen. Some things are part of our destiny, and sometimes we "know" about something before it happens. This knowing gives us reason to believe it will happen. This explains the many instances of people who believed they would be famous before they did become famous: They believed they would be famous because they "knew" they would be. They knew because Essence gave them that knowing. And that knowing inspired them to take the actions that made it happen.

Essence gives us images and intuitions of our destiny sometimes long before it manifests as a way of preparing us for it and encouraging us in that direction. A sense of destiny or inspiration from Essence helps us believe that that destiny is possible, and that belief motivates us and helps us overcome any hurdles we may encounter in achieving that destiny. Did we create that destiny with our beliefs? The ego would like to take credit for that because if we believe our desires and beliefs are that powerful, we will stay very involved with them. In fact, following the ego's desires and beliefs is more likely to take us away from our destiny than toward it.

The truth is that everyone has a certain destiny that Essence determines, not the ego. This doesn't mean your life is predetermined by any means, but some things were planned loosely before you were born. The ego has nothing to say about your destiny, but it can interfere with it and make it more difficult to fulfill. The ego does this primarily by giving you suggestions about what to do with your life. It tries to shape your life according to its goals and values, which are not Essence's. If you follow the ego, you'll probably succeed in getting what the ego wants to some extent. Meanwhile, Essence will try to bring about its intentions within the life you and your ego have created. Usually it manages to bring about its plan in some form. If you are very involved with the ego, Essence may not be able to accomplish its plan in the most fulfilling way possible.

We do create with our beliefs; we just don't create everything with our beliefs. They shape how we see ourselves and the world, and they shape how others see us. Our beliefs create challenges and help us overcome challenges, but they are not responsible for all our challenges or all the circumstances we find ourselves in. We co-create this life with something else, which has intentions for this life, and that is Essence. Aligning with Essence's intentions is what brings true happiness and fulfillment. Essence expresses its intentions through intuitions and inspiration, and it moves us through spontaneous urges and drives. It doesn't use beliefs (e.g., "You should own a house by the time you are thirty.") to drive and motivate us like the ego does, and that is one way you can tell whether you are following the ego or Essence in creating your life.

CHAPTER 4

Ask and You Shall Receive

HELP IS AVAILABLE

We are not alone. If there is only Oneness and we are an expression of it (and there is and we are), then everything we see is us. All of the different life forms were created to assist each other in their evolution. We need them and they need us. This is obvious enough in observing physical reality, where life forms are so intricately connected, but it's no less true in nonphysical realities. When we graduate from the physical reality we exist in now, we will exist in a nonphysical reality, and our purpose will be to serve both physical and nonphysical realities with whatever skills we've acquired thus far.

Until recent history, humanity lived comfortably with the notion of spirit helpers, spirit guides, and angels. Humanity depicted them in art, passed on stories about them, prayed to them, spoke to them, and gave them a voice. There have always been those who were able to see, hear, and feel nonphysical beings. For these people, nonphysical beings are as real as anything physical. To those who can see nonphysical beings, many appear to have bodies made of light instead of flesh, so they are sometimes called *light beings* or *beings of light.* They will be referred to here as *beings of light* or simply as *beings.*

The existence of nonphysical beings defies rationality because they can't be experienced with the usual five senses. Since science doesn't recognize the existence of a sixth sense, it concludes that nonphysical beings don't exist. This is understandable. If something isn't in your experience, it's logical, although inaccurate in this case, to conclude that it doesn't exist. So it's up to those who do experience nonphysical beings to describe them and their experiences with them to others.

What those who can see and communicate with nonphysical beings consistently tell us is that nonphysical beings of all kinds exist. To try to describe and categorize them would be an impossibly large task. For our purposes, it's enough to say that many different beings are involved with earth and with individuals on earth because they deeply love the earth and humankind. Many of them have had lifetimes on earth and are motivated by those lifetimes to help earth and humankind evolve.

Each of us has a number of beings working with us on a daily basis. These helpers may change over the course of our lifetime, but usually there are at least four present at any one time. These helpers have specified tasks and often work together on these tasks. Some are being trained and are overseen by others who are more knowledgeable. As on earth, these beings learn by doing, and they don't perform their tasks perfectly. They are learning and growing as they serve us.

Because their job is to help us evolve, their work often entails helping us heal the wounds and issues that can block us and keep us from fulfilling what we came to earth to learn and accomplish. However, they can't help us without some willingness and cooperation on our part. If we aren't ready and willing to be healed, they do what they can to make us ready and willing. They do this primarily by sending us people, books, or other information that will help us see the need for healing and inspire us to be open to doing something about it.

Have you ever reached a point in your life when you said, "That's it. I'm tired of being depressed (or unhappy or scared or addicted)," and you did something about it? Those are turning points that beings of light rejoice in. When people are suffering, they often become open to solutions they weren't open to before. Before that, people often don't utilize the available resources, and they can't be made to, as many social workers and others involved with helping people know. These beings can't make us utilize their help either. They have to wait for us to be willing to receive it. They wait for us to want it and ask for it. Suffering is often what brings us to this point of being open to receiving help and being open to believing that it can come from "God" or spiritual forces.

When people are suffering, they become open to new solutions: Those who were never religious before try prayer, and those who never believed in psychics and channels turn to them for answers. When life doesn't go as we would like or when we feel helpless or powerless in relation to some issue, we start asking the big questions, most of which start with "Why." These are the questions religions are supposed to have answers for and science isn't designed to address: Why are we here? Is there a God? Why is there suffering? Why is there evil? Why am I experiencing this? Why is life this way?

The answers to such questions have always been available, but not everyone accepts the messengers and therefore the messages. Because channels and psychics are not esteemed in this society, what they say is often ignored or disparaged. This is understandable to some extent, since not all channels and psychics are created equal; some are not very good at what they do. As a result, much wisdom never reaches those who need it. Beings of light await humanity's readiness and willingness to receive answers to these deeper questions.

Beings who do explain such things to those who are curious use language and metaphors to describe what is difficult to put into words. Language can never accurately describe reality, but even an approximation of the truth is better than misunderstandings. So these beings do try to reach those who are open to listening, and they attempt to provide answers that will be useful at that point in time. They have to gauge their communication to the language, culture, times, intelligence, and experience of the channel and whomever is listening. They do the best they can within the limitations that language presents.

Nevertheless, a lack of readiness or willingness to receive understanding isn't always reason enough to withhold it. Sometimes it's necessary and useful to stretch people by giving them information that causes them to see things differently. Beings of light have often played this role as well. They introduce new ideas, which is one of the ways that new ideas, innovations, and inventions come into our reality. These ideas and inventions affect the evolution of humanity and earth. These beings have played and play a much larger role in humanity's evolution than you may think. They do this primarily through psychic means: through dreams, visions, the intuition, inspiration, and channels.

Another way they do this is by becoming physical. Beings who no longer need to reincarnate on earth sometimes come to earth in the usual way (by being born) because they want to bring new ideas or inventions to earth that it needs. These individuals have been called by various names, such as *starseeds, wanderers,* and *star people.* They may also come into a body later in life as a *walk-in.* Walk-ins come into a body through soul exchange: One soul leaves the body and another comes in, usually during an illness, a coma, or a near-death experience, but not exclusively.

When such a soul exchange takes place, it is usually not remembered, and the new soul takes on all the conditioning of the previous soul, including the astrology chart. As a result, even loved ones may not be aware of the exchange. The experience of the soul exchange is often seamless, especially if it happens in childhood. However, sometimes the exchange is obvious because the change in consciousness is so dramatic. This explains some instances of spiritual awakening and high levels of consciousness functioning through someone who previously didn't lead a particularly pure or spiritual life. The consciousness of the walk-in can be so elevated compared to ordinary people that he or she appears very unusual or even God-like. Many walk-ins have exceptional gifts of all kinds, which is why they are here. A number of present day spiritual teachers and healers are walk-ins.

The reason this phenomenon is being mentioned is to help you realize that you are being helped to heal and evolve, not only by beings of light, but also by very advanced souls who have come to earth to help raise the level of consciousness here. These advanced souls are everywhere, and many are bringing in new healing techniques and information that are awakening people to their true nature by freeing them from their conditioning. Many of those who are awakening are star people themselves, who have come here to bring new ideas and other forms of help to the earth, which so sorely needs it now. You may even be one of them!

The intention of light beings and the advanced souls who have come here is to raise the level of consciousness so that wiser choices are made on behalf of the earth, which is in peril now. Beings from all over have assembled here to help humanity live more in harmony with all of life, which is necessary for humanity's survival. There's a real possibility that the earth may reach a point of no longer being able to sustain life, particularly human life, and that would be a great tragedy for it and for others in the universe. This juncture has been reached on many other planets before, where free will has resulted in people being so out of touch with the Oneness that life is affected. When that happens, the beings guiding that planet call for help, and more forces are brought to bear on the situation. This is the position the earth is in now and why healing is important. With healing and freedom from conditioning come different choices, and that's what the earth needs now.

AN EXPLANATION OF EVIL

Serving humanity and the earth would be much easier if it weren't for physical and nonphysical beings who are interfering by serving themselves. There are those on earth and beyond earth, in other dimensions, who are working at cross purposes to those who are serving humanity and the earth. They are serving themselves rather than serving the Oneness. In serving themselves, they are creating a lot of pain and difficulties for people on earth and slowing the process of consciousness acceleration that is so necessary for the earth's and humanity's wellbeing.

One of the big questions people have, which religions have tried to address, is the question of evil: what it is and why it exists. Evil is what happens when the connection to love is lost. When people (or nonphysical beings) become deeply identified with fear, greed, and hatred, they become unable to feel love or their connection with the Oneness they are part of. They become lost, in a sense. They end up so far away from Home that they don't know how to get back, and they don't even remember Home or love. They can become so lost that they don't even want to go Home because they don't believe it~or love~exists. What they believe in and what runs them are fear, hatred, and a desire for power. These negative feelings become the reason for their taking action, and actions based on these feeling are destructive. We call these destructive acts and those who perpetrate them *evil.*

Human beings aren't born evil. They come into their round of incarnations more like a blank slate, like a child who has much to learn. They become what they learn from their environment and those around them, and they become what they conclude about their experiences. In our early lifetimes, we have little wisdom and few resources for coping with life. We make mistakes and learn from them, hopefully. Over the course of many lifetimes, we develop wisdom, gain skills and inner resources, and learn to love.

What happens instead with some young souls (those who haven't had many lifetimes) is that they learn to hate, usually because they've been abused or tortured or have met with some other tragic fate. If they don't receive healing, they can become more fearful and hateful, either because they continued to receive hateful treatment or they continued to come to wrong conclusions about themselves or about life. When the wounding is so great and the resources for dealing with it are so few, an individual often reverts to extremely primitive survival behavior, in which the ego is in full sway.

The ego is out for itself and only itself. When it feels threatened, it pits itself against the world. Like an animal backed into a corner, the ego will do anything to survive and get on top. The ego sees no other goal in life but this. It is panicked and afraid, and moral behavior becomes irrelevant. This can also happen to young souls who were never taught morals or who were taught amoral or antisocial behavior. They can become so identified and aligned with the ego that love has little chance of winning them over.

When individuals are lost to love, it can be a long road back because they aren't open or willing to see love as an option. To those so deeply entrenched in the ego, love is seen as weakness, and weakness doesn't enhance survival. They see power, not love, as the answer to life and how to live it. They want power more than they want love because they believe that power will bring them everything they want. To them, love is abstract and meaningless. They don't feel it, so they don't believe in it. People (and nonphysical beings) can become so lost to love that they no longer recognize or value it.

Behavior that comes from such deep identification with the ego and with its fear and greed is bound to wreck havoc in the world. It goes against life. It takes the individual, and often those affected by it, away from love. How far can someone go in this direction? Very far. When individuals go very far in this direction and they haven't been able to be rescued, they perpetrate evil and embody it. Evil happens when we become so cut off from the Divine that there's no longer a sense of connection to it and no feelings of love.

Thus, the Divine didn't create or cause evil, but evil is allowed to exist for as long as it will. Eventually, nearly all souls find their way Home, but it takes some souls eons before they do. Meanwhile, they leave a trail of suffering behind them. So much of the suffering on earth is caused by their misguided behavior. Unlike the challenges that Essence sets for us, the difficulties caused by these lost souls are hard to heal and grow from. Essence designs challenges to develop us and lead us toward love, happiness, and fulfillment. But the difficulties caused by these lost souls interfere with people's spiritual plans and can set their evolution back lifetimes. There is good reason to work with these individuals to bring them back into the fold so that they don't continue to do damage in this lifetime and in lifetimes to come.

Unfortunately, because we are horrified by their terrible acts, we treat these individuals punitively instead of providing them with the healing they need. We treat them as if they were subhuman, when what they need most is healing. Healing comes from love, not from heaping more violence and isolation on them. Our justice system isn't oriented toward healing them, although more evolved societies elsewhere in the universe are. This doesn't mean we should allow these individuals to be free. We need to protect society by limiting their movement, while providing healing and rehabilitation before returning them to society. It makes no sense to return criminals to society who haven't been rehabilitated.

In some respects, healing needs to start with these individuals before they perpetrate more evil and bring others onto their path of negativity and self-destruction. Victims often become victimizers, especially if this happen early in our incarnations. So both victims and perpetrators need healing.

NOW NEGATIVE NONPHYSICAL BEINGS AFFECT HUMANITY

Another very large but not widely recognized factor in the perpetration and perpetuation of evil is the involvement with humans of nonphysical beings who are oriented toward serving themselves and away from love. Just as human beings can become lost to love, some nonphysical beings, some of which have never been human, are lost to love. They are acting out in the same destructive ways on their level, and these levels have an effect on humanity.

Although most people are not aware of these destructive nonphysical beings, which will be called *entities* for simplicity and to differentiate them from beings of light, nearly everyone is affected by them. Those most affected are some of the most vulnerable people in our society: those who are mentally ill, drug or alcohol addicted, suicidal, and criminals. In some cases, entities not only perpetuate these conditions, but also cause them. When human beings fall into negativity and become consumed by negative feelings, particularly fear and hatred, they become vulnerable to psychic attack from entities, who see the possibility of gaining power over them.

Entities see themselves as gaining power by manipulating others. The more people they are able to affect, the more powerful they are in their realm. And the more powerful they are, the safer they feel. Unlike here, where love protects us by joining us with others who have resources that help us survive, entities are protected from being preyed on by other entities by being seen as powerful. Those who have less power are persecuted by those who have more power.

Whole worlds exist that are based on fear and power rather than on love. These worlds are hell realms. Earth is a heaven compared to these places, where love has no meaning. Eventually, these worlds will evolve, which happens through interventions from beings of light and others whose work it is to heal these realms.

Even high functioning human beings can be affected by entities. All it takes is a certain amount of negativity, which draws entities to you and allows them to remain there. For instance, if you have thoughts of self hate, you will attract entities that resonate with that and help perpetuate those thoughts. If you have a lot of fear, you will attract entities that resonate with that and perpetuate that. Entities are part of the human condition, and as such, need to be addressed in healing the human condition. Entities don't cause the initial negativity; the ego, wounding, and other conditioning cause that. But people who are very entrenched in the ego and its negativity become magnets to entities, who make it more difficult to become free of that negativity.

Entities do this primarily by increasing the intensity of the negative conditioning. They can increase the volume of it, so to speak, and increase the frequency that it arises. When negative conditioning is unrelenting, it's very difficult to detach from. Until it diminishes somewhat, it's very difficult to ignore. Even when people know that a negative thought isn't true and it should be ignored, they may still identify with it, in part, because they lack something else to identify with. If all that's in your mind is negativity and you are strongly identified with your mind, then what else do you identify with? The negativity leaves no room for positive thoughts and interferes with the ability to experience Essence. Then it can seem like negativity is all there is and there is no way to escape it. Somehow, some positive programming needs to be created or activated to counteract the negative programming, but when the negativity is this great, someone else is usually needed to help with the reprogramming and give voice to Essence.

A very important step in this intervention, which is often overlooked by those who don't know about entities, is to send the entities away. Sending them away is not particularly difficult; even the person whom they are attached to can do this. The biggest stumbling block to ridding negativity is not realizing that entities exist and are aggravating the problem. Healing is much more difficult when entities are intact. Therefore, healing needs to be approached from two directions: Any entities that are there need to be sent away, and the negativity that allowed them to be there needs to be healed.

When you identify with a negative thought, it's like saying yes to that thought. This yes is an invitation to entities. It's like saying, "You're welcome here." And the entities are likely to stay until you say no to that negative thought. Entities can't coexist with positive thoughts and feelings. If your mind and feelings are positive, entities can't come near you. Positive thoughts and feelings create a shield of sorts that prevents negative intruders from affecting you, as long as you continue to remain positive. A little negativity isn't a problem if the negativity is short-lived and if positive thoughts and feelings are also accessible.

During times of stress, illness, emotional upheaval, and change, even people who generally think positively are vulnerable to entities, who await opportunities to influence them. Having an impact on otherwise positive-thinking people makes entities feel especially powerful. They leave these people alone only because they can't get to them. Otherwise, they are as vulnerable to their attacks as people who think negatively. Positive-thinking people bring too much love to others, and that is in opposition to the entities' goals. Because entities are out to prove that love is weakness and not a viable path, they are especially interested in bringing those people down.

Attacks on those who generally think positively often don't last very long or have much effect because the power of positive thoughts and feelings (especially love) far outweighs the power of fear and negativity. Usually those who think positively have a connection with Essence and with their spiritual helpers, which gets them through difficult times. These people gain inner strength from their challenges and are the ones who are able to lend strength to others in times of crisis, which is what makes them especially prized by entities. Some of these people know about entities and know how to fend them off and send them away.

Knowledge is power. Ignorance of the existence of entities allows them to operate secretly. Knowing about them gives you the power to evict them and send them on their way, hopefully toward the Light (love). Beings of light do this for us when we ask them to. They also attempt to do this without our awareness; however, without our cooperation and agreement, it isn't as easy. As long as entities have a foothold because of some negativity, they are likely to remain unless that negativity is healed.

The negativity needs to be healed *and* the entities need to be sent away. Healing the negativity would be enough, but it's often difficult to do that while entities are still there maintaining the negativity. To be successful, healing needs to be done in conjunction with sending the entities away. Any negativity that is strong enough to have entities maintaining it is going to need more than positive self-talk or talk therapy to heal it. The most persistent negative thoughts and feelings need work on a psychic level as well.

Nearly everyone has or has had entities attached to them. They are a major factor in the perpetuation of human suffering. They magnify the programming we were given. The programming itself is not so much of a problem because some of it is neutral and even positive, and there are spaces between our conditioned thoughts, where Essence is able to break through. However, programming can become a real problem, a prison of sorts, when it is magnified by entities. They don't magnify all of our conditioning, just the conditioning that resonates with them. This conditioning drowns out other potentially helpful thoughts. Positive thoughts often don't stand a chance in relation to these negative ones because they loom so large.

The persistence of these negative thoughts wears people down. They feel helpless, powerless, and hopeless in the face of such negativity. Many who are clinically depressed are in the grips of this phenomenon. Talking to them isn't enough to draw them out of their negativity. Drugs work for some because they change the brain chemistry in a way that allows for more positive thoughts and feelings. Drugs give the person a break from the negativity so that they can begin to think more clearly again. Unfortunately, however, drugs don't expel entities, and many attract them.

People who are drug or alcohol addicted are magnets to entities, who not only exploit them, but also get some pleasure from their drug use. Some entities that are attached to people, particularly to addicts, are disembodied humans who were addicted in their former lifetime and are trying to continue their addiction. They plant thoughts in people's minds that encourage them to abuse alcohol and drugs. They represent a voice of temptation that can be difficult to argue with.

Entities torment addicts in other ways as well. They tell them they are worthless, life is hopeless, no one cares, and whatever else the entities think will cause them to either continue to use drugs or alcohol or commit suicide. Entities gain power in their realm if they can manipulate someone into committing suicide. They figure that suicide is proof that they have convinced another of the viability of their path. Usually, however, those who commit suicide are taken to "hospitals" by beings of light to heal and reorient their understanding, and suicide is rarely repeated. People learn from their mistakes once they are out of the body more effectively than when they were in the body.

In addition to magnifying our conditioning, entities can insert themselves into our mind in the form of a negative voice. They choose carefully what they say, playing on our weaknesses, desires, and current troubles. For instance, if your husband left you for someone else, an inner voice might tell you that you are worthless and your life is ruined. Or it might suggest ways of handling the situation that anyone would term bad advice. It spins a sad and terrible story that generates negative feelings that entities feed on. This manipulation through thought is very common, and often very little objectivity is brought to it. If this voice were examined more carefully, it could be seen for what it is; however, many people don't examine their thoughts before acting on them. This is especially true of younger souls, who are most vulnerable to entity attachment and manipulation.

ASKING FOR HELP

Life brings us the understanding, insight, courage, and determination we need to overcome our conditioning, but often not before we ask for it. Essence allows us to experience as much suffering from our conditioning as it takes to get us to want to be free of it. Suffering brings us to the doorstep of Essence, then Essence frees us.

One reason asking for help in healing conditioning is important and necessary is that it acknowledges the problem and our desire for a solution, which shows a readiness on our part to become free of our conditioning, or a piece of it. Without that readiness, help isn't likely to be that helpful, whether it comes from helpers in a body or outside a body. Asking for help may seem too simple to matter, but it's actually a very big step in the healing process.

Asking shows not only that we are aware of a problem, but also that we have some understanding of it. To be aware that something is a problem, we have to have noticed that it's caused problems for us. This noticing is Essence, pointing out the effects of our conditionings. What else would do this? Not the ego, whose job it is to maintain conditioning. Something other than the ego is working to guide and shape your life, and it manifests within you as awareness, wisdom, insight, and the will to change and heal. And it manifests outside of you as helpers in all forms.

When we open up to help from Essence and from helpers to heal our conditioning, help arrives. That is the meaning of, "Ask and you shall receive." This statement doesn't mean we'll get everything our ego desires and asks for. It means that when we ask for help or healing or for what Essence intends for us (e.g., love, growth, peace, wisdom, understanding, clarity, fulfillment, happiness), we'll receive it, although it may not come in the form we expect or desire.

Asking doesn't need to involve a ritual, but rituals are often helpful in solidifying our commitment to being free of our conditioning, which is why rituals are a long-honored tradition. Performing a ritual in conjunction with our request to be free of something affirms our willingness and readiness to be free, most importantly to our unconscious mind, where our conditioning is stored. Rituals mark endings and new beginnings, and they send a signal to our unconscious mind that we are no longer willing to be run by that conditioning. Such conclusive statements make a mark in the unconscious mind and weaken the conditioning. Rituals can also help create and reinforce a new self-image that is free of that conditioning. They can be a way of reprogramming the unconscious mind with new, freer images of ourselves. As a result, it becomes easier to choose the new self-image and behavior over the old.

A ritual doesn't have to look any particular way. In fact, one designed by you is likely to be more powerful than one taken from a book, but anything will do that allows you to feel the power and presence of Essence. The powerfulness of any ritual comes from evoking Essence, from calling forth the Divine and asking to be aligned with it. Doing this helps you begin to see yourself as divine and powerful and able to be free from the ego. Rituals empower us. They give us the strength to be who we really are. They help us affirm what is true, good, and real and turn away from what is false.

Another aspect that adds power to many rituals is the presence of other people, who help each other align with Essence and witness each other's request and commitment. Not only is there power in numbers, but the presence of others also helps create a clear delineation between the past and present. Rituals, such as weddings and funerals, have served this purpose throughout time. They mark passages from one phase of life or phase of being to another. They cause us to think of ourselves and our life differently, and that's all that healing really requires.

Could healing really be as simple as replacing old images with new ones? Yes, this is very much what heals conditioning. After all, conditioning is just thoughts. When we replace negative thoughts with new, more positive ones, healing happens. What inspires us to create new images of ourselves and, in fact, gives us new images is Essence. Where else would positive self-images come from? They come from outside our conditioning and outside our ego, which maintains conditioning. They come from Essence to free us from the egoic trance and awaken us to our true nature.

The beings that work with you know who you really are and they know who you *think* you are. They know best how to help you see the truth. They show us the truth of who we are many times a day, but we don't always notice. Every day we get glimpses of our true nature and how we might live in the world as that. Every day there are opportunities to live as Essence rather than as the ego. Some of these opportunities are taken, and some are passed by.

Healing is important not only to ease our suffering, but also to ease the suffering of others because once we are free of our conditioning, we can't help but want to help others become free as well. You are here to make a difference in the world, but your fullest impact can only be made by living from Essence, not from your conditioning. When you ask for help for healing, you are joining with many, many others, both physical and nonphysical, who are also committed to healing and helping. This is a request that can only bring you joy.

To ask requires some humbling. What is humbled? The ego, of

course, which is another reason why asking is powerful. Asking is admitting the inadequacy of the ego to guide your life and bring you happiness, and that opens you up to receiving what you need from Essence. Asking puts you in a receptive mode, which allows you to experience and hear Essence. The ego's mode is active: It tries to shape life according to what it wants. But the truth is that the ego has only so much power to do that. In the end, Essence shapes our life, and we either go along with it or resist it.

Once you ask, your role is to allow and receive. You allow Essence to play its part, which it has been waiting to do. And you allow the beings working with you to do theirs, which they have been waiting to do. And you see what happens. You put yourself in their hands and trust that they know what to do. You don't have to understand what they are doing or how they are doing it; you just have to be willing to receive what they are offering. Asking is the most important step, then allow others to help.

CHAPTER 5

Clearing Negativity

CLEARING ENTITIES

The good news is that the biggest hurdle to getting rid of entities is not knowing they exist. In most cases, entities aren't difficult to get rid of, and nearly anyone can clear them. In fact, it's a good idea to clear them periodically, since they tend to come back during challenging and stressful times. Whenever ego-identification and emotions are strong, entity attachment can recur. Entity attachment can happen even to those who are very advanced spiritually. They remain vulnerable to entities because ego-identification can still happen, and when it does, entities are more than willing to try to keep that identification and those negative feelings going.

What is most important to understand is that entities are not powerful, not in this realm or in any realm. The only power they have is what we give them by believing them or by believing they are powerful. They actually feed on negative feelings, especially fear, meaning they grow in confidence and brazenness when negative feelings are present. Fear and other negative emotions allow them to have an influence on our consciousness, while love and other positive emotions drain them of confidence and repel them.

If you are doing a clearing by yourself, you need to be free from fear and negativity and in a positive state of mind to be successful in dispelling the entities. You need to feel confident, safe, and protected and aligned with all that is good. Calling on beings of light to protect you and help you align with all that is good is a good way to begin any clearing. Even if you aren't able to remain positive, entities can't harm you in any way other than the ways they have. But they may not be convinced to leave if you, yourself, aren't able to believe in the power of love and express a commitment to it.

Being positive can be a challenge. If you've been living with a lot of negativity, you may not feel love or the presence of loving spiritual forces. You may have taken on the entities' point of view to the extent that it makes it difficult to feel positive feelings and align with a more positive viewpoint about yourself and life. If that is the case, it may be necessary to work with a healer who is used to doing this kind of work and who can help you get to the bottom of some of the negative beliefs that have allowed the entities to be there. Once you do this work with a healer, perhaps a few times, it will be more possible to do it on your own.

Entities are easy to send away, but the same entities or others are likely to come back if you haven't done some work on the negativity (mistaken conditioned beliefs) that attracted them and allowed them to be there in the first place. You may be able to uncover these beliefs yourself through inquiry and release them, or you may need some help from a healer to do this.

Healers who are intuitive or psychic and who can receive information from the beings that are working with you are best able to do this work. This is most often the work of shamans and those who call themselves energy healers or energy workers. If you are intuitive, you can probably discover most of the underlying beliefs yourself. Some of them may be connected to a past-life or more recent trauma that may need to be addressed and released energetically. Beings of light will do this for you when you ask them to. Healers are also helpful in clearing these patterns.

How to Clear Negative Entities

The process of clearing entities is three-fold: Once you have quieted your mind and moved into a peaceful and positive emotional space, call in the beings of light (which include angels) who do this type of work, ask for their protection and assistance in clearing any negative entities, and affirm your willingness and readiness to receive their assistance.

Second, ask for insight into what allowed the entities to become attached. Answers will arrive through your intuition or through the healer's intuition who is working with you. Answers could come in the form of insight, knowing, images, or words.

Third, once you realize what beliefs underpin the negativity, ask the beings of light to help heal those issues.

You may need to repeat this process regularly, at least for a while, to reinforce and maintain the healing and prevent the entities from returning. The specific words you use during this clearing aren't important. Your intent is what is responded to by both the beings of light and the entities. The intent to clear the entities sets the process in motion and brings about whatever needs to happen.

For this process to be successful over time, it's important to maintain positive thoughts and feelings as much as possible every day. This will strengthen your ability to stave off intruders and establish a new, more positive, way of thinking. The clearing process may seem magical, but it isn't magical in the sense that it isn't instantaneous or without the need for effort and commitment on your part to ongoing healing and developing a more positive mind. Here is an exercise to help keep you clear of negativity:

Exercise: Staying Free of Negativity

Whenever you find yourself caught in negative thoughts or feelings, ask beings of light for assistance in clearing that negativity. Also ask for assistance in uncovering any beliefs that underlie the negative feelings. Take time to be quiet and listen for answers to what beliefs caused the negative feelings. What did you say to yourself that made you feel that way?

Stopping the snowball of negativity before it gets bigger and inquiring into the cause of your negative feelings puts you in a new relationship to your thoughts and feelings—one of a curious observer of your thoughts and feelings rather than identification with them. This is a very big step in overcoming and managing negativity. Negativity gains a foothold in our consciousness because we let it by following its line of thought: One negative thought leads to another and another until an upsetting story is created. Stopping this before the negativity builds is much easier than trying to stop it later.

WORING WITH ANGELS

The beings of light most dedicated to this kind of healing work are angels. They have never been human, but they act as guardians of the human race and others like us on other worlds. Angels have a deep understanding of what we call evil, and it is their mission to transform it. Their work involves rescuing those who've turned away from love and lost their way. Sometimes they assemble in large numbers to convince wayward souls of the power of love. At other times, just a few are all that's needed. The strength and number of entities attached to someone varies quite a bit. Angels bring to the situation whatever numbers are needed. Strength in numbers alone tends to be very convincing.

Entities are very familiar with angels and other beings of light, who often approach them and try to rescue them. However, entities have been told not to trust angels and other light beings. Entities believe that going into the Light with them will lead to their demise, and it does. The transformation they undergo is dramatic and permanent. Once entities go into the Light, they never return to their former existence.

Fear is what keeps entities doing what they do. They are afraid of other entities who have more power. More powerful entities have lied to them about the nature of the universe. These entities don't realize they are lying; they are just passing on what they've been told. All entities believe that the Light is a place of dissolution of all will and therefore power. They can't imagine happiness, love, or peace because they've never experienced them, so the promise of these is empty. As a result of these lies, entities are afraid of angels, which is why entities do listen to angels when they tell them to stop what they are doing. Some entities, mostly those with little power, decide that going into the Light can't possibly be worse than their current plight, and they go with the angels and are pleasantly surprised. Many of the beings of light working with angels were once lost souls.

Angels are available the instant you call on them. They are in touch at all times with all life that comes under their guardianship. You can call on them mentally or out loud for anything at any time. No request is too small. Angels view us as their children and rush to our care, especially when called on. They monitor our thoughts and behavior and send love and blessings our way. When we are open to receiving their love, we feel it; when we aren't, we can't. They wait patiently until we are ready and then shower us with love. Usually, we receive a mere droplet of what they have to offer. This love is what heals and evolves us. It is the divine nectar that brings all souls Home. The more we are open to it, the more we receive it. It's also called Grace.

The human condition results in being cut off from awareness of the realms where beings of light reside. A lack of belief in these realms closes us off to receiving their help because beings of light aren't allowed to intrude on our free will. If we choose to not believe in angels or in other dimensions, beings of light allow us to have this experience until we choose differently. Free will can take us so far away from love that it becomes difficult to come back. People can become very lost in greed, selfishness, hatred, fear, and other negative states. Turning this around may require some dramatic interventions. Accidents, illnesses, losses, and other crises often serve to wake people up to looking at life differently, but how much easier it would be if the choice to move away from love hadn't been made in the first place.

Moving away from love happens not because human beings are naturally bad or evil, but because they lack wisdom (which takes lifetimes to develop) or because they've been wounded in a way that leaves them cut off from love and in the grips of fear. Life has a way of healing our wounds and making us wise, eventually, because it is designed to do this. We can speed this process along by understanding how life does this and by summoning and being open to the resources that life has to offer.

Life heals us by bringing us circumstances that show us what we need to see about ourselves and our conditioning. It stirs up our conditioning so that we become aware of it and the effect it has on our life. It does this largely through our relationships with others, whose conditioning we often come in conflict with. What we do when conflict arises determines whether our conditioning will be healed or continue to function as usual. We can choose to blame, judge, try to change, fight with, or avoid the person who stirs up our conditioning, or we can take responsibility for it and investigate it.

Angels and other beings of light can help us take responsibility for our conditioning and heal it if we ask them to. Whenever your conditioning arises, you can ask for help from angels and other beings of light. Instead of trying to change others, you can ask for help in changing yourself. Doing this is more powerful than you may realize.

This is a very different relationship to life than usual. It's the difference between the ego's relationship to life and Essence's. The ego goes to battle with the way life is showing up, while Essence accepts the way it is showing up. To accept life, you have to be willing to see that the problem is not what is happening, but the fact that you don't like what is happening. If you liked what was happening, it wouldn't be a problem. To be rid of the problem, you have to stop seeing whatever is happening as a problem. This is an amazing revelation, which will change your life: You don't have to change life, only your relationship to it, your attitude toward it. Angels can help you do that.

Calling on Angels for Help

Angels and the other beings of light working with you are trying to help you become free of your conditioning. They do this in two ways:

First, they can help you see life as Essence sees it. They can help you see life more positively. The way they do this is through your intuition and by planting positive thoughts in your mind.

Second, angels can help heal your conditioning by working on you energetically.

When we ask for healing, angels pour Light into the places in our energy field that need it. Our energy fields have places where the energy congeals, which represent emotional complexes. Our fields also have tears that make it possible for entities to attach to us. Angels untangle the complexes, remove the entities, and fill the holes with Light. They know exactly how to do this, and they don't need anything from us except a request to have it done. All we have to do is call on them, and they do the repair work energetically. Although our energy field will eventually return to its previous shape if our thoughts and emotions don't change, this repair work can give us enough temporary relief from our patterns to make it more possible to change our relationship to our thoughts.

Our intuition is the voice of goodness, of Essence. The mind, on the other hand, is generally the voice of the ego, which promotes selfishness and fear. For those who have a very developed intuition, it resembles a positive voice and may even appear as a voice in the mind. In every moment, we are presented with two possibilities: to follow the ego's voice or Essence's. For many, the ego's voice wins out because it's stronger and more obvious. As we evolve, Essence's voice strengthens. Because it's not as accessible as the ego's, we have to make an effort to hear it. We have to use our free will to free us from the domination of the egoic mind. We do this because we've become tired of the suffering caused by the ego and because we've come to trust that there's another wiser voice available to guide us.

Our intuition is our connection with the beings of light that are working with us on a daily basis and with other beings of light who show up from time to time to help us in other ways. They may be assisting us in creating something, such as a book, a movie, or a piece of art or music. Or they may be guiding us in bringing in new information that helps humanity in some way, such as new healing techniques, inventions, and progressive ideas that uplift society. Beings of light inspire us and move evolution forward through us, and they do it through our intuition, which is their primary means of communicating with us. They also communicate with us through dreams, although not every dream is a communication from them. Beings of light use our intuition and the intuition of others to bring us information, insight, inspiration, encouragement, and creative ideas. What we create and accomplish of a positive nature begins with them.

Beings of light are entrusted with the job of motivating us to fulfill our life plan and helping us do that. They inspire us to move in a particular direction and provide us with the information and insight we need to learn our lessons and fulfill our destiny. They are able to influence others through their intuition to help or hinder us. They steer us through life by providing opportunities here and roadblocks there. They shape and sometimes limit our possibilities to keep us moving in a direction aligned with our life plan. They do this through intuition, inspiration, and urges. For instance, they can inspire us to pick up the phone and call someone. We can always say no to these urges, but often we don't. They can and often do save our lives in more ways than we realize by urging us or others to do or not do something at a particular moment.

Because we have free will, we don't always follow through on these urges or intuitions. What most interferes with following them are our ideas about ourselves or life, our conditioning, and the ego's desires, which can be at odds with Essence's plan for us. When we follow the ego's plan instead of Essence's, we can end up very unhappy and depressed. Many live miserable lives because they have lost touch with what Essence intended for them.

Fortunately, it's always possible to return to Essence's plan, although it may require some very big changes. Crises of all kinds are often used to bring us back into alignment with our plan. Crises cause us to reassess our lives and what is important to us, and they shake up our life structures, making room for new ones. Although times of crisis are not easy, they can feel very enlivening and rewarding because they often bring us back into alignment with our life purpose and with what is most meaningful to us.

We all have a life purpose that is spelled out very generally before we come into this lifetime, while the specifics are decided as we go along in life. The specifics are determined by the opportunities presented to us (which beings of light have a hand in) and by the choices we and others make. Beings of light do what they can to put us in places and situations that are conducive to learning what we came to earth to learn and doing what we came here to accomplish. Whether we succeed or not is up to us. Beings of light have only so much power to influence us. They allow us to make choices that take us away from fulfillment because they know we will learn from those choices. We often discover what really makes us happy only after doing what we *think* will make us happy. Beings of light understand this and allow us to walk our journey as we choose, while offering us guidance and insight every step of the way.

We all have equal access to help from these beings. The only limiting factors are not believing they exist and not asking them for help. Because we become more capable of perceiving them and communicating with them as we evolve, their help naturally becomes more available. Those who can communicate with them can help others who can't. These beings often work directly through psychics and channels to bring those who don't have easy access to them the messages, information, and encouragement they need to learn their lessons and fulfill their life plan. But there is one hitch: Nonphysical beings who are out to serve themselves and disembodied humans, who are not always so wise, can also communicate through psychics and channels, so discrimination is important.

You can tell the difference between beings of light and beings who are out to serve themselves by their tone of voice and the content of their messages. However, many who are out to serve themselves go to great lengths to imitate beings of light: They talk about love and use terms of endearment in speaking with us to win our trust. So we are left with having to evaluate the content of the message very carefully.

The biggest difference between beings who are serving themselves and beings of light is that beings of light don't offer specific advice or tell you what to do, for example: "You should move to Portland." "You should leave your husband." "You should buy that stock." "Go to that restaurant, and you'll meet someone." "Quit your job." "Go on a fast." Telling you what to do is an infringement of your free will, and beings of light are very careful not to do that. They may make suggestions, but they don't tell you to do something specifically. You are here to exercise your free will and learn from that. Unfortunately, many people are looking for just such advice and are willing to take it from anyone who pretends to be worthy of giving it.

For some of these beings, this is a way of feeling powerful and having fun, while others are sincerely trying to be helpful. There is quite a range of beings involved with psychics and channels, all the way from manipulative and deceitful to well-meaning but unqualified to benevolent and wise. Some well-intentioned psychics and channels are unknowingly involved with beings who mean no harm and who are attempting to be helpful but don't have the skills or knowledge they need to be helpful. These beings offer all kinds of specific advice and information, which may or may not be helpful or true. The fact that some of it is useful keeps people who are looking for someone to tell them what to do coming back. The truth is that only the answers within you, from your intuition, or Heart, count. Beings of light give you specific guidance about what to do through your intuition, not directly.

Another difference is that beings who are out to serve themselves often provide information about the future that flatters you or makes you feel special. They are also willing to give you information about others behind their backs, which beings of light won't do. Beings of light don't gossip about or tattle on others, but some beings are happy to do that if you're looking for that. Beings who interact with people this way are skilled at reading people's desires and weaknesses and playing on them. They bond with people by telling people what they want to hear and pretending to have information they want.

If beings of light give you information about the future, it will be very general and positive. They don't tell you about something bad that is about to happen or say anything that will frighten you or make you feel bad about yourself. They are always supportive, but they don't feed your ego. They help you see yourself and life more positively, more truly. They bring you Essence's perspective and any understanding that will help you be a better and happier person. And they lead you toward love, not away from it.

UNTANGLING EMOTIONAL COMPLEXES

Angels untangle emotional complexes on an energy level, but for the energy to remain untangled, the mistaken beliefs that created the tangle of energy need to be erased or reprogrammed. This is done by first getting in touch with the mistaken beliefs and then replacing them with a truer perspective. Once the falseness of these beliefs is seen and they are replaced with a truer perspective, the emotional energy that these beliefs generated, which also held them in place, dissipates. Then new behaviors become established based on this truer perspective, and the healing is complete.

These complexes are what get triggered by other people's conditioning. Conditioning triggers conditioning, and that's how everyone's conditioning gets healed eventually. When an issue is triggered, it usually causes an automatic emotional response. Any number of negative emotions may get triggered, which is why it's called a complex. It's made up of many hidden beliefs that trigger a variety of emotions. Unless these beliefs are investigated, the usual circumstances will continue to trigger the conditioning. Furthermore, the more this complex is triggered, the more entrenched and automatic the emotional responses become. The responses become habitual, and habits aren't so easy to break. To break this cycle takes a conscious choice and willingness to investigate the ideas behind the feelings, which is what heals the emotional complex.

To heal an emotional complex, it is necessary to allow the feelings to be there without responding to them in the usual ways. These feelings are the trail that leads you to the goldmine of understanding. They contain the answers you are looking for, which will free you from your conditioning, but acting out your feelings will take you away from that goal. So you sit with these feelings and wait for them to reveal the mistaken beliefs that are the cause of your unhappiness and your so-called problems. These beliefs are things such as, "Life should be different," "Life is unfair," "I will never be loved," and "I'm flawed and will never be happy."

Beliefs like these are sad and inaccurate conclusions your ego came to when it faced disappointment, disillusionment, and pain. They are a story the ego told about an event, and the ego became attached to that story and created an identity around of it. It concluded something that wasn't true, but it believed its conclusion.

To admit that its story isn't true is very difficult for the ego. It is very attached to its point of view and doesn't want it questioned or examined. The ego will come up with all sorts of reasons why you shouldn't bother to investigate your feelings and your beliefs. The ego will try to talk you out of doing it because it doesn't want you to see the truth, because if you do see the truth, you won't need the ego and the identities it gives you.

Once these beliefs are seen as false, they stop driving your behavior, and then more positive beliefs can take their place. Some negative beliefs literally disappear, never to appear again. Others remain but are a mere shadow of their former self, without the ability to convince you. Eventually, they too will disappear if you don't decide to resurrect them. What allows you to see these beliefs is an attitude of curiosity, gentleness, and acceptance. In just being with the emotions that are tied to them, they reveal themselves quietly, intuitively, one by one.

Being with an emotion is an act of not doing: You don't think about the feeling, and you don't act on it. You just wait, listen, and receive. You are very present to the feeling, as if it is all that exists in the world. You give your full attention to it, without an agenda and without straining or trying. You bring gentleness, curiosity, and acceptance to the feeling, and that compassionate relationship to the feeling allows the beliefs behind the feeling to be revealed. What you are waiting for is not so much a thought, but a knowing, an insight, that pops into your awareness, which may have an image or a sensation attached to it. Intuitions often come in the form of images or sensations that deliver a sense of knowing, which afterwards are translated into words. The longer you sit with an emotion, the more beliefs are likely to be revealed, since beliefs are linked together, just as emotions are.

To understand this better, let's look at an example. A woman reacts with disgust and judgment toward her husband whenever he expresses his anger or even a strong opinion. The reaction is out of proportion to the incident and not limited to her husband, so this is a sign that something unconscious has been triggered in her. So she sits with these feelings of disgust and judgment and lets them speak to her. She discovers that her husband's anger and strong opinions also cause her to feel afraid because they seem violent to her. An image of rape, perhaps something that happened very long ago in some other lifetime, comes up. She experiences the shock, helplessness, and anger of the woman she was back then as she was overpowered by a man. At that time, her anger and words had no impact on him, so she concluded that being angry and speaking up was useless, even dangerous. She also concluded that power was ugly and cruel. She never wanted to be powerful if being powerful meant that.

The unconscious mind takes these conclusions as orders and shapes our behavior accordingly. So in this lifetime, she is soft-spoken, gentle, and accommodating. Her style is to go along with others and not rock the boat, until something triggers this issue, when she becomes the angry one who throws her weight around. Repressed anger has a way of either seeping out or surging out.

When people have been the victim of abusive anger, they do two things: They repress their anger when it isn't safe to express it and they express it in times of stress over little things or in situations where it seems safe to do so. At these times, they can become what they didn't want to become: overpowering and abusive. They are stuck between two polar opposites: disowning their power and abusing their power. Once they realize they have a negative relationship to power, they can begin to establish a healthier relationship to it.

In this example, a new relationship with her personal power is called for. She can ask beings of light to help her express true power rather than power as the ego wields it. True power comes from alignment with Essence and what is real. The ego's power is power over oneself and others. It's an attempt to manipulate life according to its ideas. True power doesn't act on the basis of ideas and desire, but on the basis of love, wisdom, and compassion.

Insight into an issue is really just the beginning of healing, although a very important first step. Once you've uncovered the beliefs, or conclusions, that underlie the feelings that get triggered, you can ask for healing around those beliefs from beings of light, which will come in the form of love energy and further insight and guidance about that issue. The complex will continue to unravel over time as you continue to see the truth about it and replace your old behaviors with new ones. This process of healing is not instantaneous, but can take quite a while, even with the help of beings of light.

CLEARING NEGATIVE SELF-IMAGES

Self-images are just images, ideas, but they can have a powerful impact on our lives and on our happiness. They can limit us by limiting what we are open to. If some activity doesn't fit our self-image, we don't do it. If we can't see ourselves doing something, we don't do it. This is fine in many cases, but there are times when doing something that doesn't fit our self-image is exactly what we need to do to be happy or to learn something new or to grow. Because we are creatures of habit and don't easily take on new self-images, we often choose to be true to our self-image rather than stretch ourselves and experience something new.

Part of the difficulty is we don't even see we have a self-image. We have many self-images, really. Different ones show up depending on what we are doing and who we are with: Around our kids, the image of the parent we think we are shows up; around our spouse, the image of the spouse we think we are shows up; around our employer, the image of the employee we think we are shows up. Around one person, we pull out one self-image; and around another, we pull out a different one. We like to be around people who bring out a self-image we like, and we don't like being around people who bring out a self-image we don't like.

The truth is we have so many self-images we can't even keep track of them. They show up and disappear as quickly as a thought. So, as important as our self-image is to our happiness, it's really nothing more than a thought that is constantly changing and often inconsistent from one moment to the next: One moment we are the good parent and the next moment we are the terrible parent.

Most of our self-images aren't useful because they are narrow and limiting and because they aren't true. They are caricatures of ourselves that leave out what is most important: our true nature. A true self-image would be true from one moment to the next. It would be good for all occasions, for every moment. The only self-image that can live up to that is one that resembles your true self, one that exemplifies the qualities of Essence.

A self-image that reflects the qualities of Essence would certainly be a positive self-image. What would be better than having an image of yourself as loving, lovable, kind, generous, patient, wise, compassionate, accepting, and every other good quality you could name? What would that be like if that were your self-image? If you are going to have any self-image, then let it be that one. All others are useless. This is a self-image that can really serve you. It will evoke the qualities of your divine nature and help you live them. You naturally express these qualities when you drop into Essence.

Expressing these qualities is the purpose of all of our lifetimes and of spiritual evolution.

It is actually possible to be all of these qualities because that is our natural state. What a wonderful discovery! You have actually always been lovable, loving, good, kind, compassionate, wise, and accepting. The only thing that has ever interfered with realizing and expressing those qualities is the ego. Once the ego and all its negative and limiting self-images are set aside, what is left is a very positive, and true, self-image. It couldn't be truer that you are every good quality you can imagine. Healing the negativity and your negative self-image is really only a matter of seeing who you really are and expressing those qualities.

Exercise: Becoming Your Truest Self

If you have difficulty imagining you are all of the good qualities of Essence, then just pretend. Try on this very positive self-image for size. If you hold this positive image long enough in your mind, your behavior will begin to reflect those qualities. Pretend you believe you are lovable, loving, kind, and accepting, and soon you will start behaving that way. If you don't believe it, try out the opposite: See yourself as mean, angry, unfriendly, critical, and you will soon start behaving that way.

Energy follows thought. You become what you believe about yourself. For example, if you believe yourself to be capable, you will naturally prove it; and if you believe yourself to be incapable, you will be discouraged before you even try.

Self-images are powerful shapers of behavior, but many other things shape our behavior and our life as well. Someone can have a negative self-image and still be very successful as a result of certain talents and opportunities. Someone can also have a very positive self-image and still have many difficulties in life, such as broken relationships, illness, and failure. As important as a self-image is, it isn't the only thing shaping your life. Your life is, more importantly, shaped by your life plan, which is orchestrated as much as possible by beings of light whose job it is to do that. Your free will, which is influenced in part by your self-image, and other people's free will also shape your life. Life is complex; it's much too simplistic to think you create your reality with just your thoughts. Your thoughts affect your life, but your thoughts aren't responsible for everything you encounter in life.

Some self-images are more functional than others. The more positive a self-image is (i.e., the closer to the truth of who you really are it is), the more functional it is. A positive self-image is always more functional and therefore preferable to a negative self-image. Does it matter if your self-image matches reality? Not really. We live up to whatever self-image we have: If it's positive, you'll live up to that; if it's negative, you'll live up to that. There's no reason not to have a positive self-image and to ignore all negative ones. We cling to our negative self-images because we think they are realistic, and we don't want to be seen as unrealistic or foolish. But it's never unrealistic or foolish to see yourself as good, kind, loving, accepting, and wise. This is a positive self-image that will never let you down.

The ego offers many other positive self-images that may not be realistic. It imagines itself to be powerful, successful, and able to have everything it wants. It puffs itself up with fantasies of being special and having an amazing life. This is an inflated self-image, not a positive one. An inflated self-image isn't positive because it isn't true. A positive self-image is dysfunctional when there's little reality to it.

Most of the positive self-images the ego offers are images of ourselves in the future. These are guesses at what will be—fantasy images. Fantasy images aren't useful self-images because they lack reality. They aren't true now, and they may never be true, unlike the image of our true self, which is always true. Investing ourselves in an image that isn't true only takes us farther from what is true and real. If Essence intends that particular fantasy to become real, it will bring it about, not through fantasizing, but by other means. On the other hand, if that fantasy isn't part of your life plan, fantasizing about it will only bring you disappointment and pain.

Self-images of ourselves in the future aren't useful not only because they aren't real, but also because they take us away from what is real and true now. What is true now and always is that your true nature is goodness and that you have everything you need to be happy right now. What is also true is that you don't know what will happen and you aren't in control of that to a large extent. You don't create your reality with your thoughts. Essence co-creates it along with your free will. The more closely aligned your free will is with Essence's, the happier and more fulfilled you'll be. However, if you use your free will and energy to create and uphold the ego's self-images, you'll have little left over to devote to Essence's intentions for you. To fulfill Essence's plan, the only self-image that is necessary is the image of your true self.

So there are two types of self-images generated by the ego that can be detrimental to our freedom: 1) limiting self-images that are based on conditioning, and 2) fantasies, which are based on desires. These images intervene between us and life. They mediate between us and others. Without our self-images, we would interact more purely, more spontaneously, and more lovingly with the world. With them, every action is checked first for compliance with the image before acting. Self-images keep us tied to the ego because they are thoughts, and when we're identified with our self-images, we're identified with the false self, not the true self.

Often we are not even conscious of having a self-image, so the first step in freeing ourselves from our self-images is to become aware of them. Here are some suggestions for doing that:

1. When you see yourself in the mirror, what do you think to yourself? What do you conclude about yourself based on your appearance (e.g., "I'm over the hill." "I'm a goddess." "I'm not living up to my potential." "I'm fit and healthy")? Answering this question will show you how your ideas about your physical appearance affect your self-image. If you like what you see, you probably have a positive self-image that coincides with that; if not, you probably have a negative self-image, at least some of the time. If a negative physical self-image is undercutting your ability to feel positive, stop giving that negative self-image the power to do that and start giving yourself the love and acceptance you deserve. Talk to yourself as Essence would. Love yourself as Essence does. Or better yet, see Essence in your eyes and know your own true beauty. Gaze at your eyes in the mirror and fall in love with That. Focus on the beauty of the Divine as it lives through you, and you will feel beautiful.

2. When you see yourself in your mind's eye, what do you look like? Do you look cross, smiley, juvenile, old, irresponsible, playful, mischievous, cool, sexy, fearful, stiff, bored, responsible, serious, relaxed, free, prissy, dorky, haggard, mousy, gorgeous? However you see yourself is probably being conveyed to others. How do they see you? How would they describe you?

3. When you are talking with others, what do you tell them about yourself? What words come after "I am"? Is yours a story of "Woe is me" or "I am fantastic" or something else? What you tell others about yourself can be either how you actually see yourself or how you want others to see you. Either way, your conversations with others reveal the self-images you hold dear. Notice how hollow and empty these stories about yourself feel, because they represent only one aspect of yourself, and a false one at that.

4. Make a list of your self-images. Think of all the various ways you see yourself, give them names, and write them down. Some possibilities are: The Princess, The Jock, The Loser, Mr. Aloof, Miss Picky, The Angel, Poor Me, The Bitch, The Sweetie Pie, The Playboy, The Glutton, The Pretty Girl, The Femme Fatale, The Handsome Devil, The Sophisticate, The Elite, The Clown, The Dreamer, The Artist, The Snob, The Law Breaker, The Intellectual, The Lover, The Spiritual One, The Wimp, The Caretaker, The Mommy, The Responsible One, The Recluse, The Warrior, The King, The Baby, The Philosopher, The Authority, The Judge, The Rule Enforcer, The Lazy Boy, The Rebel, The Complainer, The Drama Queen, The Health Nut, The Trouble Maker, The Scared Child, The Lonely One. The possibilities are endless. Some self-images are more problematic than others, but all of them are just ideas about yourself, and none represent who you really are. The self-images that have negative emotions attached to them probably need to be investigated and the underlying false beliefs uncovered. Giving your self-images names makes it easier to see them as images and not identify with them. Your humanity is made up of one self-image showing up after another, but your divinity remains the

same. Amidst this parade of images, your divinity looks on, unchanged.

Even when you have seen through the self-images that represent your astrology and your psychological makeup, you are left with self-images that are so deep-seated that you may not even consider them self-images. These are the images of yourself as a man or a woman and as a human being. These, along with the mental image of your physical self, are the most fundamental images. Once all the self-images that represent your conditioning, psychology, and astrology have been seen for what they are, there remains the need to see that you are also not your gender or your body, and you are not human.

What does it mean if you aren't human? You aren't a physical being after all, but a part of the Oneness manifesting as a human being. You aren't human. Let that sink in, and see how much the image of yourself as a human being keeps you from seeing and living as that which you truly are. You can be alive on this earth and function perfectly well without identifying with the belief that you are a human being or a man or a woman. Start realizing that these, too, are just images. You are beyond all images, even these. You are divine!

You don't have to change anything about your self-images; you only have to recognize them for what they are and then drop into the truest self-image. When you catch yourself involved in a self-image, you can learn to see yourself from the perspective of Essence. When you look with Essence's eyes on the character you are playing, you are immediately outside this character. From this perspective, there is only beauty, and all self-images dissolve.

CLEARING NEGATIVE THOUGHTS

Negative thoughts eventually weaken if you don't give them your attention. The problem is that some negative thoughts are difficult to ignore. Those are most likely to involve feelings, particularly fear. Any fearful thought is quite difficult to ignore because we generally believe that our fearful thoughts help keep us safe. However, when we examine this belief, we see how very little truth there is to it. Most of our fears never manifest, not because thinking about them prevented them, but because our fears are generally not grounded in reality. They are just thoughts about some future possibility.

The ego generates fears as a way of keeping us tied to it. The ego generates fears and then a plan to avoid those fears, which is unnecessary and useless. We can waste a lot of time and energy worrying about and planning for things that never happen. Essence has ways of protecting us from whatever we aren't meant to experience. It protects us in moments of danger by guiding us intuitively to do what we need to do to be safe. As for things we are meant to experience, there's little we can do about those, but bring Essence to them when they occur. A good rule of thumb is: If it's a fear, it isn't worth your attention. All fears come from the ego, and these thoughts, like so many others, aren't good guides for how to live our life.

Other thoughts that can be difficult to ignore are thoughts about the past that are charged with feelings. Some investigative work might need to be done around recurring thoughts that relate to a traumatic or difficult event. But for the most part, ignoring them as best you can will cause them to arise less frequently and with less intensity. On some level, we think we can change the past by thinking about it, but thinking about the past has no value, and it takes us out of the present where all is well and all is always well.

Analyzing a troubling experience from the past can stir up more emotions and keep us tied to it. Any investigation of the past needs to done from the standpoint of a curious and accepting witness (such as Essence). Experiencing an event from the standpoint of a bystander can diffuse the emotions, lessen their occurrence, and heal the past, while re-experiencing an event as the victim makes it more real and keeps the emotions intact. Traumatic past-life experiences need to be worked with in the same way, as we will see in the next chapter. If troubling or traumatic events from the past can't be experienced as a bystander who is able to bring compassion, acceptance, and understanding to the situation, these events shouldn't be returned to at all.

Exercise: Clearing Negative Thoughts

Our deepest conditioning tends to come up the most. Whatever negative thoughts you think the most point to your deepest complexes, which are likely to need some investigation and healing. Make a list of the thoughts that most plague you and leave you feeling unhappy about yourself. Those are the ones that especially need healing.

These negative thoughts also need ignoring. The more you are able to just let negative thoughts come and go without reacting to them emotionally (identifying with them), the weaker they will become, until there is little emotion left to them. Thoughts that are just thoughts and have no emotion attached to them are easy to ignore with a little commitment to doing that.

It isn't necessary to analyze or go to battle with your negative thoughts. This is the mind's way of dealing with negative thoughts.

The mind can be used to unravel the mind through investigation, but arguing with a negative thought or over-analyzing it from the level of the mind isn't useful. It only brings you into greater involvement with the mind, not less. The reason to do this work is to lessen your involvement with the mind, not increase it. Going to battle with conditioning ensures that it will remain strong: "What you resist persists," as the saying goes.

The antidote to conditioning is acceptance, but the mind isn't what can give acceptance. Acceptance happens when you drop into Essence and notice your negative thoughts. From Essence, negative thoughts aren't a problem because you see that they have nothing to do with you—the real you. When you don't identify with your negative thoughts, they have no power to stir up feelings or motivate your behavior. It's as if they belonged to someone else. If someone else were having these thoughts, would they be a problem for you? Of course not. That's how it is when you are identified with Essence. You have compassion for the suffering such thoughts cause, but they don't cause you to suffer.

However, if you are having difficulty ignoring or being detached from a thought, try putting your attention on something truer:

Exercise: Directing Your Attention to the Now and Away from Negativity

When ignoring a thought seems difficult, then don't try. Instead, turn your attention onto something beautiful or onto a sound or sensation—onto the experience of the moment. Become very attentive to what is arising in the present moment, and thoughts will automatically drop into the background, unless you start thinking about what you're experiencing rather than just experiencing it.

Thoughts take you out of the present moment into another time—into the past or the future. What about now? What's happening now? Check it out. Experience what is happening right now. You may be surprised. Something delightful is always happening in the Now. Find it and experience it.

The mind leads you to believe that you have a problem and life is troublesome and difficult. That's the mind's take on life in nearly every moment. The truth is much better than that, much brighter. For those who can see from Essence's eyes, there is much beauty available in every moment. Turn your attention to the present moment, and watch your thoughts disappear into the nothingness from which they came.

CHAPTER 6

Using Past-Life Regression to Heal

THE BENEFITS OF PAST-LIFE REGRESSION

Past-life regression can free us from old emotional, behavioral, and attitudinal patterns that block us, and it can help us get in touch with the aspect of ourselves that has lived many other lifetimes. Past-life regression may be necessary to heal deeply entrenched issues that are rooted in a previous lifetime. When a painful past-life experience hasn't been able to be integrated because we are locked into feelings of fear and powerlessness generated by the trauma of that experience, past-life regression can free us from these feelings and help us integrate the experience. Here are some additional benefits of past-life regression:

- It demonstrates that we are more than we appear to be.

- It provides an explanation for our behavior, fears, drives, needs, compulsions, or problems, which helps us accept and heal them. Past-life regression helps us understand our responses to life that are unreasonable, unexplainable, compulsive, inappropriate, and out of proportion to a situation.

- It has been successful in alleviating depression, anxiety, phobias, psychosomatic illnesses, metaphysically-based illnesses, certain skin problems, asthma, gastrointestinal problems, high blood pressure, and headaches.¹ Sometimes dramatic improvement of physical symptoms results.

- It brings feelings out into the open where they can be acknowledged and accepted.

- It gets the unconscious and conscious minds working together toward greater wellbeing.

- It increases creativity and intuition by activating and helping to integrate the right and left hemispheres of the brain.²

- It can be used to access positive states in past lives. It can help us access personal power, inspiration, and other resources.

To benefit from past-life regression, it isn't necessary for you to believe past lives are real. Past-life therapy is effective whether you believe the images are actual images from a previous lifetime or just something conjured up by your unconscious.

WHO CAN BENEFIT FROM PAST-LIFE REGRESSION

We all have had traumas in our past lives, and yet we don't all need past-life regression. Besides the possibility that we may no longer have any traumas lingering in our unconscious, we may not need past-life regression because healing a particular trauma is not on

---

[1] Raymond A. Moody, Jr., M.D., *Coming Back: A Psychiatrist Explores Past-Life Journeys* (New York: Bantam Books, 1992), p. 113.

[2] Karl Schlotterbeck, *Living Your Past Lives: The Psychology of Past-Life Regression* (New York: Ballantine Books, 1987), p. 216.

our soul's agenda for this lifetime. What trauma or traumas are chosen to be worked on in a particular lifetime depends on our other lessons, the karma to be released, and whether working through that trauma fits with the rest of our life plan.

When healing a past-life trauma is on our soul's agenda, the psychological issue or issues that stem from that trauma will be portrayed in the astrology chart. When a lifetime is to be focused on healing an issue from a former lifetime, the chart may be chosen expressly for this. However, not all past-life issues are significant enough to warrant this. Nevertheless, because every chart will be chosen to address some psychological issue, if not one stemming from a trauma, careful reading of the astrology chart can pinpoint problem areas and indicate a direction for any healing work.

When an entire lifetime is focused on releasing a difficult issue from a former lifetime, that issue may consume most of our energy. Difficult issues like these can shape and distort our perceptions and interfere with our wellbeing and growth. The overwhelming nature of these issues calls for therapy. Most people in this situation aren't equipped to work through these issues on their own.

The kinds of issues that present themselves as overwhelming are often the result of more than one traumatic experience. It's common for someone who has experienced a trauma in one lifetime to try to overcome it in another by facing it again, only to reinforce the fear instead of eradicate it when it's reencountered. This can go on for several lifetimes. When a fear has been reinforced, it can be particularly hard to work through. It may manifest as a phobia or, more commonly, be cloaked in neurotic or compulsive behavior that interferes with functioning and happiness.

Whether a psychological issue is caused by a past-life injury or a current one isn't always obvious. Many who seem wounded but who have had perfectly normal childhoods and supportive parents may be suffering from pain from a previous lifetime or lifetimes. For them, past-life regression may be in order if the wounding is interfering with their functioning. Others who have experienced wounding in their childhoods that reinforces past-life injuries and who are making little progress in therapy also may be candidates for past-life regression if the reason for their lack of progress is that conventional means haven't been able to reach to the problem's root. Whenever difficulties are particularly resistant to psychotherapy, past-life regression may be in order. Obviously, when psychotherapy is sufficient, past-life work isn't necessary.

One way to determine whether past-life regression is right for you is to consult with a channel who can supply information about past lives and what is needed. Channeling is one means by which information of this nature can be obtained. However, care must be taken to find a channel who can reach levels of intelligence capable of delivering accurate past-life information. Reading past-life records isn't easy, and only evolved beings can do this accurately. A good channel may also be able to provide information about other healing options. Some channels even channel regressions themselves.

If you have determined that past-life regression may be helpful to you, here are some criteria for evaluating your readiness for it:

First, you need to be able to relax, so some familiarity with relaxation techniques or meditation will be helpful. Second, you need some ability to visualize. Are you able to see images during guided visualization exercises? Not everyone is strong in the visual mode; some people are more auditory and kinesthetic, and will relate better to hearing and feeling than to images. Those who are auditory or kinesthetic can still benefit from past-life regression, but they also have to have some ability to visualize. This ability can be developed with the help of the many visualization materials on the market. Learning to visualize will take time, but if you are willing to pursue this, it can be well worth the effort. Visualization exercises, alone, have many benefits.

The final criterion is whether you are willing to commit several sessions to past-life regression. It sometimes takes months of weekly sessions to heal and integrate a trauma from a former lifetime. You need to stay with the process until results are achieved.

WHAT TO EXPECT

Before having a regression, it's important to know what to expect. If you don't fully understand what to expect, you may back out when the going gets rough, which it often does. Because many of our troublesome behaviors, attitudes, and feelings are means, although ineffective ones, for coping with the fear and other negative feelings created by a trauma in a past lifetime, nearly all regressions will bring us face to face with a traumatic experience. Going back to a traumatic incident and viewing it as if it was happening to someone else helps you integrate it and overcome its negative impact.

In past-life regression, the past incident is not reproduced as the victim experienced it because doing that would only reinforce the fear. It's re-experienced from the standpoint of a witness or, in some cases, from the standpoint of the soul or even the perpetrator. This is an important difference not only in the experience's level of intensity, but also in its healing effect. The observer has resources that the victim didn't have, and is able to view the incident objectively, as if it was someone else's story. The observer not only learns from observing the incident, just as we learn from the characters in a movie, but he or she is also often able to feel compassion for the offender.

This insight and compassion are possible because other elements of the story unknown at the time of the offense are revealed to the observer. If you can gain insight into the aggressor during the regression, you may even experience that soul's response to the harmful act and understand how deeply disturbing it is to that individual's growth. From this higher perspective, you'll be able to move from the fearful, powerless position of a victim to a place of understanding, compassion, and forgiveness. So the shift from victim to observer (or to the soul) empowers you by enabling you to transmute fear into compassion and understanding, which are the gifts of the painful experience.

There are past-life therapists who have success allowing their clients to re-experience the feelings of the victim instead of just witnessing the event. Their success can be attributed to their knowing how to work through the feelings that arise in the regression and their commitment to doing that. Any emotions that are re-experienced in the past-life regression must be worked through with the usual therapeutic methods. The method presented here of keeping the person in the witness role is one way of doing past-life regressions that is safe even for those who are not skilled at working through feelings.

During a past-life regression, images from a previous lifetime will emerge from your unconscious as if you were watching a movie. Events will just unfold of their own accord as you watch. Feelings will also emerge. You will have a sense of having been there before or of remembering something you once experienced. Sometimes there are feelings of nostalgia as you watch the scene unfold. The images can be quite vivid, unlike a daydream.

When the painful incident begins to unfold, you should just watch it without reacting emotionally to it, as if you were sitting in a movie theater, watching an interesting plot unfold. The feelings that will arise are those a moviegoer would experience—excitement, suspense, concern—but they won't be the same as the protagonist's. You'll be aware of the feelings of the other characters in an equally objective way. Moreover, if you ask for it, you'll receive insight into what the events mean to the souls of those involved. The therapist will be busy asking you questions to keep you on track and help you uncover the necessary details.

Although the regression won't be a duplication of the initial experience, it may still be uncomfortable at times. Even as an observer, you'll feel some of the victim's discomfort, just as anyone watching a disturbing event would. The pain we want to avoid in a past-life regression is the pain that comes from becoming the victim again. This can be difficult to avoid because the tendency throughout the regression is to return to this role. When that happens, even briefly, the victim's pain will be felt.

The initial session may be only the first step in moving beyond the fear, pain, and anger to forgiveness. It may be necessary to return to the incident several times before you experience it objectively. Each time you return to it, you'll come away with more understanding and readiness to forgive. Once you've managed to feel some forgiveness, you are well on your way to healing the experience. You must be patient with this process. It sometimes takes several sessions before an issue is dealt with sufficiently. But with perseverance, integration can be achieved.

The fact that past-life therapy may take several sessions before its goal is achieved is not a reflection of its ineffectiveness, but of the strength of the ego, which insists on maintaining its defensive feelings of fear, pain, and anger. The ego is a mechanism of survival, and fear is one of its means of defense. When the ego feels threatened, fear helps it mobilize its other defenses and alert us to future threats. However, when fear is inappropriate or out of proportion to the circumstance, it robs us of energy and prevents us from functioning as fully as we can. Then fear becomes a detriment rather than a help. This is the kind of fear that lingers into the next lifetime after a trauma. It is an automatic, conditioned response that, instead of protecting us, inhibits our functioning.

The only way to eliminate these fears is to go back to the cause, and the only way to do that is through imagery. The unconscious can be asked to make the painful experience available to the conscious mind through imagery. Once the painful experience is made available this way, new resources can be brought to the experience, making it less overwhelming. This is the theoretical basis for past-life therapy.

HYPNOSIS AND LIGHT TRANCE

A past-life regression can be performed in an ordinary state of consciousness, a light trance state, or a deeper hypnotic state. The deeper the trance, the greater access there is to details, dates, and other specifics, but these details are not always important to the healing process. Usually a light trance is sufficient, although many have success working with people who are neither hypnotized nor in a light trance.

One of the reasons for working with people in either a non-hypnotic or light trance state is the resistance to and fear of hypnosis that many people have. Given this, it might be useful to dispel some of the myths about hypnosis:

- It's not dangerous.

- You don't lose consciousness during hypnosis. Hypnosis is a deeply relaxed state, a state of heightened awareness.

- You can't be made to do anything against your will.

- Hypnosis is not a truth serum. People sometimes lie and make up things under hypnosis. [3]

During hypnosis, we feel a sense of deep relaxation in which we have no desire to move, a sense of detachment from our surroundings, a heaviness and numbness in the limbs, and a sensation of floating. [4]

The method of past-life regression presented here uses a light trance state. There's nothing mysterious or paranormal about this state. We experience it while driving, watching television, and doing other repetitive activities that require little conscious attention. Anyone who can experience a light trance state can have a successful regression, given proper preparation.

AN INDUCTION FOR PAST-LIFE REGRESSION

Here is an example of an induction for a past-life regression that induces a light trance state and sets the stage for the regression. It's presented to give you an idea of what an induction is like. It's not suggested that you try to use this alone to induce a regression. You will need someone with experience to guide you:

Breathe deeply and slowly, and relax into a comfortable position in your chair. Feel the softness of the chair beneath you, and feel yourself sinking deeply into its softness. All you have to do is relax and listen to my words.

---

[3] Raymond A. Moody, Jr., M.D., *Coming Back: A Psychiatrist Explores Past-Life Journeys* (New York: Bantam Books, 1992), p. 180-181.

[4] Ibid., p. 181-182

We're going to take a journey back in time to a place you once knew. It will be like visiting a familiar place, but you will have the sense that you are watching yourself in this familiar place instead of being that individual. There may be times when you find yourself becoming that individual, but try to just observe that individual. It will be like watching a story unfold, except that you are at the center of the story. This story has already happened and is over and done with. But by paying close attention to the details of the story, you may discover something that will help you.

As the story unfolds, remember that we can stop or change the action anytime if we need to. You don't have to experience painful feelings. We will stop or change the action before you feel anything painful. You are in total control of this experience.

Let's begin by boarding the train that will take you back in time to this faintly familiar place. As you board the train, you know that each step is a step closer to your destination. When you arrive in the train's compartment, you look around for just the right seat. Slowly and deliberately you walk toward this seat and sit down. From here, you can see the countryside outside the window.

As soon as you are seated, the train begins to move: slowly at first and then gradually picking up speed. You gaze sleepily out the window and watch as the countryside becomes a blur of colors. The clackety, clackety sound of the train as it moves over the tracks lulls you, and you feel a deep sense of relaxation and calm. The train continues on through the darkness of the night and on into the early morning, when the colors return and the sunshine makes its appearance again.

You are aware that today you will reach your destination. Today you will meet with a long lost aspect of yourself that needs your attention and comfort. You have chosen to take this journey to help this part of yourself. That part has been lost and isolated from your awareness, and soon it will meet you for the first time and be healed.

As we near the station, the train begins to slow down. Slowly the colors begin to take the shape of trees, landscape, houses, and people. As the train slows to a stop, the focus becomes clearer. You rise to disembark. You feel a sense of expectancy and anticipation about what is waiting for you. As you step down from the train, the scene unfolds.

Take all the time you need to allow the scene to unfold. If you allow sufficient time, a story will unfold that will reveal the lost aspect of yourself. This aspect of yourself is eagerly awaiting your recognition. When you have some sense of a scene, tell me about it so that I can be there too. Don't be afraid to tell me even the smallest detail because even it may be important.

After the induction, the facilitator draws out the imagery the client is experiencing and reminds the client to just observe. What happens in the past-life regression depends largely on the imagery that arises.

Certain themes emerge repeatedly in past-life regressions. Pursuit is one of the more common ones. A pursuit is often taken to the point of capture and the action stopped before the trauma is inflicted. At that point, the individual would be asked to identify either what the aggressor is thinking and feeling or what the aggressor's soul is experiencing.

Another possibility is that the pursuit is changed into a game and the pursuer into something harmless before or at the point of capture. Usually this technique of rewriting the story, called *re-scripting*, would not be used unless remaining objective was a problem. More will be said about re-scripting shortly.

Another option that can be an especially effective way to reinstate the victim's power is to rewrite the pursuit, allowing the victim to become the pursuer and the aggressor, the pursued—without the tragic ending. The result can be comical ("Oh, I thought you were someone I knew"), practical ("Here, you dropped your keys"), or friendly ("Aren't you someone I knew at Washington High?"). This neutralizes the fear and puts the victim in charge.

Because powerlessness is a common theme in past-life regressions, rewriting the story to allow the victim to either be in a more powerful position or experience an inner sense of power (by witnessing the action) can be an effective tactic. Feelings of powerlessness and hopelessness lingering from past traumas can be as immobilizing as fear. So when powerlessness is an issue, role reversal can help. However, rewriting the story this way is usually not sufficient to heal past-life wounds. It generally needs to be followed by replaying the original trauma and observing it.

HEALING TRAUMATIC DEATHS OR VIOLENCE

Many pursuits end in death or violence. It may not be necessary to re-experience the violence or the death (as an observer, of course) to clear it from the unconscious, but sometimes these moments must be faced and worked through. The facilitator needs to be intuitive and experienced enough to know what's needed.

In general, if the death or violent act took place quickly, it's less likely to need to be faced than one that was slow and extremely painful, either physically or emotionally. Also, if pain lingers even after having dealt successfully with the pursuit, then the trauma itself will probably need to be re-experienced. If work with the pursuit was sufficient, you'll feel relieved and relaxed; you may even laugh.

When viewing a violent or deadly event, it's especially important to just observe it. If you identify with the victim, the action should be stopped and restarted. One technique that might be used during a death scene to help you maintain objectivity is to have you speak to the victim during the traumatic experience, much as Essence or a guardian angel might speak to him or her in such a circumstance. The facilitator might direct you to do this by saying something like this:

Now, be her (his) guardian angel and talk to her. Tell her how much she is loved. Tell her she will always exist, that no one can destroy her spirit. Tell her that she did all she could and that she can't change what is happening to her now. Tell her that her death is something she must accept and that her loved ones are waiting for her on the other side. Ask her to forgive the pitiful individual who is doing this to her, who is hurting his (her) own progress by this. Then as the observer, say goodbye to her as she leaves her body and enters another dimension.

Many death experiences don't need to be healed; every lifetime ends in death. When death is part of a natural conclusion to life, we feel no trauma or lack of acceptance. Usually only accidental, sudden, or traumatic deaths create psychological damage that will need to be dealt with in the future. The extent of the damage depends on the attitude at death. Some examples of traumatic incidents that may warrant past-life regression are attacks by people or animals, transportation or machinery accidents, falling or drowning, natural disasters, rapes and other violations of one's person, political or wartime atrocities like torture and imprisonment, and death on the battlefield.

Whether a death results from these incidents or not, the trauma may leave its mark. Incidents resulting in death aren't necessarily more traumatic than those in which we survive. Often the opposite is true. It can be more devastating to survive and live with the memory and results of trauma than to escape its haunting in death. Nevertheless, the memory of most traumas can't be escaped even in death, for the memories live on in our unconscious and are reflected in our psychology in future lifetimes. This may seem unfair, but it's just the way life is.

A violent act or death will most often be a problem in future lifetimes if a detrimental feeling or belief has become programmed into the unconscious along with the trauma. We usually draw conclusions related to our feelings of powerlessness, shame, guilt, hatred, or fear at the time of the trauma. These feelings and conclusions become connected with another element in the story or with our sense of self and bleed through into the current lifetime.

For example, if a red-haired man was the perpetrator in a former lifetime and feelings of powerlessness and disgust were associated with that experience, then each time the former victim encounters a red-haired man, he or she may re-experience those same feelings. Whenever strong negative feelings can't be explained by circumstances in the current life, their origin may be in a previous lifetime. Or, if we died traumatically as a result of our own poor judgment, we may distrust ourselves without understanding why.

HEALING PHOBIAS

Fears about objects, activities, places, or animals also often have their origin in past-life traumas. Sometimes these fears, or phobias, are so great that they keep us from functioning normally around the feared object. Phobias are easily alleviated through past-life regression. Once the fear's origin is pinpointed, it's just a matter of speaking to what is feared in a Gestalt-type dialogue during the regression. In these dialogues, the client gives voice to both the victim and what is feared. The following is an example of this:

Client: "Snake, why did you make me fall off the cliff?"

Snake: "I didn't make you fall. You weren't looking where you were going. I just wanted you out of my territory. You didn't have to back up."

Client: "Where was I supposed to go? There was nowhere else to go."

Snake: "I don't know. I don't think of these things. I act by instinct, and my instinct was to scare you away by striking at you. I'm sorry you had to die, but that's life."

Client: "Well, that's easy for you to say. You didn't die."

Snake: "What can I say? These things happen."

Client: "Yes, I suppose they do. I guess you're not so bad. You were just acting instinctively."

Facilitator: "Can you forgive the snake for acting like a snake? Maybe you could tell it that."

Client: "I forgive you for doing what snakes do."

Facilitator: "How does that feel?"

Client: "A little silly, but it feels better... reasonable, but I still feel sad."

Facilitator: "Can you forgive yourself for making a mistake that ended your life? Try saying, 'I forgive myself for falling off the cliff.'"

Phobias can sometimes be healed in one session, although further work may still be needed around the sudden or violent death or accident.

Guilt often also becomes associated with a trauma. This is especially true if we witness a traumatic incident and can't prevent it from happening or if we feel responsible for it. When guilt is connected to something about the incident, compulsions may arise from it. Compulsive washing, for instance, is often an attempt to cleanse unconscious feelings of guilt associated with a past-life trauma. Or, the compulsive act may be related to the actual scene that produced the guilt, as in the case of a man who paced back and forth compulsively because this is what he did along the edge of the fault line where he watched an earthquake swallow up his family.

Like guilt, shame and feelings of worthlessness resulting from rapes and other similar traumas may also become stored in the unconscious if they aren't healed. In future lifetimes, these feelings can lead to promiscuity, impotence, fear or shame around sexuality, or further victimization.

Another common theme in past-life regressions is witnessing another's trauma or death. The most traumatic instances are those involving a loved one in which the witness was powerless to help. These situations can be particularly traumatic if the witness was under duress as well, for instance, if he or she was also captured and tortured or forced to watch a loved one suffer. In these instances, remaining an observer may be especially difficult, since that was the position during the tragedy.

Instead, traumas like these can be worked through by having the witness speak to the lost loved one during the regression and express the sorrow and guilt that didn't have a chance to be released. This common Gestalt technique, known as *the empty chair technique*, is effective for both past-life and current loses. It may be all that is needed to work through painful experiences such as these. In these cases, as in others, much of the healing occurs just by making what was unconscious conscious.

Sometimes, however, the witness of a tragedy also was involved in its perpetration and continues to be haunted by this. For them, forgiveness is the key to healing. They need to speak to those they have injured and express how they feel and ask for their forgiveness. Then they need to forgive themselves by stating this out loud. Rewriting the story or just witnessing it isn't necessary or appropriate in these situations.

RE-SCRIPTING

Instead of witnessing an incident as you experienced it in a former life, your past-life therapist may have you rewrite the story while you are re-experiencing it. As the old story is replaced by the new one, fear is replaced by whimsy or some other emotion. Re-scripting can provide lightness and humor, which help us go beyond the seriousness of the moment. Humor has a way of distancing us from a painful situation, just as witnessing it does. This is why humor and laughter are healing. If a painful situation can be transformed into something comical, it becomes less personal and poignant. This is what we hope to accomplish in past-life regression so that the intensity of feeling created by the initial incident is neutralized and no longer bleeds through into the current lifetime. The following is an example of this technique:

Facilitator: "Now what does she see?"

Client: "I see a man."

Facilitator: "Remember, be the observer: she sees a man. And what is he doing?"

Client: "He's coming after me! I'm afraid!"

Facilitator: "Now, stop the movie. Just relax and take some slow, deep breaths and listen to my voice a moment. Remember, you aren't this girl—you're watching this girl. The girl you are watching is frightened. What can we do to change these feelings? Do you have any suggestions? What would make her feel better?"

Client: "She'd feel better if it was just a game—like tag."

Facilitator: "Okay. Let's see what that would be like. Let's go back to the story where we left it and pretend that they're just playing tag, and tell me how that feels."

Client: "He's running and she's running. She's running fast, but he's still catching up because she's just a kid. He's going to catch her! I don't like this game!"

Facilitator: "Okay. Let's stop the action again and try something else. What else would take the scariness out of this game?"

Client: "If he were smaller, weaker, or more friendly."

Facilitator: "How do you want to picture him then?"

Client: "Like a playful puppy. I want him to be a little puppy chasing her, wanting her to play."

Facilitator: "Alright. Let's go back to the story where we left it and change him into a playful puppy and see what happens."

Here a life-threatening situation has been turned into a game and then a romp with a puppy. This incident will be reprogrammed in the unconscious and stored safely away as a harmless romp with a puppy. The reason this works is that the unconscious operates like a computer. Stating that we no longer want the memory stored as it was is a clear command to this computer, and asking it to replace the bad memory with a good one makes it easier for it to do that.

Re-scripting is only used when the witness technique has been unsuccessful, that is, when objectivity and forgiveness haven't been achieved. The witness technique is preferable to re-scripting because more insight and understanding can be integrated. Re-scripting is useful for neutralizing the painful emotions before trying the witness technique again.

THE WITNESS TECHNIQUE

The following example illustrates the value of the witness technique:

Facilitator: "What's happening?"

Client: "I'm in a dark alley. Someone is approaching me—a man. He's stumbling around like he's drunk. He doesn't see me yet. I'm trying to get up, but my leg hurts too much and I can't move. He's coming closer. My heart is pounding."

Facilitator: "Stop a moment and remember that you are not this girl. You are just observing her. You see she's frightened and can't move. What does she do?"

Client: "She curls up in a ball, hoping the man won't see her. That's comforting to her, like if she doesn't see him, then he won't see her."

Facilitator: "What happens next?"

Client: "He stops and bends over her and shakes her shoulder to see if she's awake. She's frozen with fear and doesn't move. He starts laughing and pulls her up to a standing position. Her leg hurts! Then he starts kissing her and grabbing at her clothes!"

Facilitator: "Okay. Stop here. Address the man who's doing this. Address him as yourself, not as the girl. Ask him why he's doing this, as if you were a reporter doing an interview. Remember, this is just a story, someone else's story."

Client: "Why are you doing this, and what are you feeling now?"

Facilitator: "What does he say?"

Client: "He says, 'Who are you? Get outta here! I'm just havin' a little fun.' Can't you see she's hurt and scared? She doesn't want you to touch her."

Facilitator: "What does he say?"

Client: "He says, 'I wanna see her squirm. It excites me.' Leave her alone, you brute!"

Facilitator: "That's fine, but don't get personally involved. Respond as if it's only a story with no reality to it. Ask him what he thinks will happen if he carries out his desires. How will he feel?"

Client: "I'm just curious, sir, how will you feel after you have satisfied yourself? He says, 'I don't care. It doesn't matter. Nothing matters. Leave me alone.'"

Facilitator: "Let's go back to the girl and see how she is doing."

Client: "Something funny is happening here. The girl isn't so scared anymore. She's beginning to see him as the pathetic character he is. She sees him as weak, not strong, and she's beginning to feel strong inside herself, not physically strong but courageous."

Facilitator: "Do you think you could write another ending to this story now?"

Client: "Yes."

Facilitator: "Let's do that."

If the action had been stopped at the critical point and the aggressor turned into a clown, for instance, the individual wouldn't have had the opportunity to experience the situation from a more courageous perspective. The transformation that took place rewrote the story itself without the need to create a different, more humorous ending. The insight that was gained may seem insignificant from the intellect's standpoint—anyone can see the aggressor is a pathetic character. However, having this realization in a light trance state can be very healing because it reprograms the experience in the client's unconscious. As a result, that memory will no longer evoke feelings of powerlessness, but inner power and strength.

ACHIEVING ESSENCE'S PERSPECTIVE

The perspective of the souls of those involved was not introduced in this example because it wasn't necessary. The following takes the same scene and shows how the perspective of the souls or guardian angels of those involved might be used to accomplish the healing:

Facilitator: "What's happening now?"

Client: "He's kissing her and grabbing at her clothes."

Facilitator: "Stop here a moment. Now pretend you are the aggressor's guardian angel. What is his guardian angel trying to tell him?"

Client: "It's telling him to stop. It's telling him it's wrong to do this."

Facilitator: "Is he listening?"

Client: "No, he doesn't seem to hear."

Facilitator: "What I want you to do is to try to experience the part of him that knows that what he's doing is wrong. Try to align yourself with that aspect of him. When you feel you have done that, let me know by lifting your right hand. (Pause) Alright. What does it feel like to be that aspect of him?"

Client: "It feels peaceful. It's loving and understanding toward him. It's trying to help, but it accepts his weakness. It feels compassion for him."

Facilitator: "Continue to see the aggressor from that perspective. Feel the acceptance and compassion. (Pause) Now become the observer again. What do you see?"

Client: "I see a frightened girl struggling with a cruel, ignorant man."

Facilitator: "Do you feel any different viewing this scene than you did before?"

Client: "I feel softer, gentler about it."

Obviously, the dialogue won't always go this smoothly. It may take several sessions before Essence's perspective is experienced. However, each session will come closer to that goal. Don't underestimate the power of this technique. It's easy to dismiss this work as silly or irrelevant, but it isn't. Working with the unconscious this way can result in healing on deep levels.

COMING OUT OF THE REGRESSION

Being brought out of the regression smoothly and gradually is important. This is usually done with a guided visualization similar to the induction. Here is an example:

Now let's return to our present day reality by boarding the train that brought you here. See yourself getting on the train, step by step, and finding your favorite seat. As you become seated, the train begins to move, first slowly and then picking up speed. Speedily it is returning you to what you know as your current reality. You feel yourself moving quickly through time, forward through time, moving quickly toward your destination in this room. The train is slowing down now, and you're nearly ready to disembark. Taking all the time you need, slowly bring yourself back to this reality and to this room. You can open your eyes whenever you feel ready.

Although the success of a regression is sometimes dramatically apparent during the regression, other times the result won't be known for a while, since most past-life work continues to have an impact subtly and increasingly for months afterward. To complicate matters, even if changes have occurred, they may be difficult to articulate. If progress is suspected, the issue may be set aside for a month or so, after which it can be reevaluated. However, if there was resistance or a lack of objectivity during the regression, further preparation or past-life work is likely to be needed.

Time does heal. In days gone by, time was often the only healing method available. Fortunately, today we don't need to wait for time to do its healing. There are ways to speed healing up. We have psychotherapy to free us from unconscious fears through awareness and verbalization, and we have extrasensory means to provide insight into the causes of our fears and compulsions. But past-life regression can resolve issues from the past even more quickly and effectively than awareness, verbalization, and insight combined. Past-life traumas that would normally take several lifetimes to heal can be healed in less than one lifetime with past-life regression.

CHAPTER 7

Tools for Moving from the Ego to Essence

LOVE HEALS

Love heals because it is our natural state. Moving from the ego to Essence heals because from Essence, all is well and no problems exist. A lack of healing is a lack of ease with oneself and life. This dis-ease is a sign of identification with the ego, and it is an ongoing and unrelenting attribute of this state. Usually, we try to heal the dis-ease by changing our circumstances or changing ourselves. That's the ego's solution to the dis-ease, which it creates. Another solution is to move out of egoic consciousness into Essence, where there is no dis-ease and no problem. However, some healing is often necessary to make this movement possible, but it's not the same kind of "healing" the ego offers.

The ego tries to heal us by changing whatever it doesn't like about us or our life or changing whatever it feels stands in the way of achieving its goals. This doesn't result in healing, but in greater entrenchment in the mind and ego. When we pursue the ego's goals, they take us farther away from Essence because they are contradictory to Essence: While Essence is the experience of unity and love, the ego seeks control and power over others. While Essence is the experience of peace and acceptance, the ego seeks more, better, and different than whatever is present. Healing requires a desire for what Essence offers rather than what the ego offers. Many of us really don't want peace, acceptance, and love more than we want what we want, that is, until we do.

At a certain point in our evolution, a shift happens and what we want loses some of its pull and glamour, and we begin to long for what is true and real; we long to experience our true nature. Getting what the ego wants is a little like eating too much candy: The more we have, the less satisfying it is. Eventually, we've had enough. We look around to see if happiness is really possible. If we're lucky, we notice that some people are truly happy. They have a look about them and a freedom that is alluring and mystifying. We begin to seek what they have found. And so the spiritual search begins.

At first, for many people, the spiritual search is a continuation of the search for happiness as the ego defines it. The only difference is that they are seeking spiritual means for getting what they want, for becoming a more successful *me*. Eventually, spiritual seekers realize that getting a better *me* isn't the way to happiness because the *me* (the ego) is still there, causing all the problems it ever did. But spiritual means—meditation, yoga, breath work, dream work, psycho-spiritual healing work, creativity, dance, singing, reading spiritual books, astrology, Tarot, and so many other tools—do get spiritual seekers somewhere. These tools help heal conditioning and the emotions, making it possible to experience Essence and break identification with the ego.

Spiritual tools such as these can free us from the illusions and misunderstandings spun by the ego. They are a means for healing, a means of experiencing who we really are and learning to move from the ego to Essence. In this chapter, we are going to explore a few ways of moving into Essence. It's easy to say, "just move into Essence and all will be well," but doing that isn't so easy at first. With the help of various tools, moving into Essence becomes much easier, and Essence eventually becomes your ordinary state.

MEDITATION

Meditation is the most powerful tool for experiencing Essence and for learning to move from the ego to Essence. It's the only tool you really need, although others serve as well. Meditation is also the most accessible tool, since it requires nothing but taking time to be quiet. To meditate, it isn't even necessary to be in a quiet environment because sounds, themselves, can be the subject of your meditation.

Meditation is simple to do, and it doesn't require much time daily. The problem is the ego doesn't like to meditate. The mind comes up with all sorts of excuses and reasons for not meditating. When you first start to meditate, you are up against this resistance and up against a mind that's been allowed to run amok for so long. It's been used to having your attention, and all of that attention has added to the mind's power and strength. Meditation is designed to diminish the mind's strength by putting your attention on something else, something truer than the ramblings of the mind.

This something that is truer is Essence, and it's subtler than thought. Essence may not even be recognized at first as anything because the mind thinks of it as nothing. Once you turn your attention away from your thoughts, you'll experience who you really are, but you might not recognize it for what it is, and it might not be experienced very strongly at first.

People often get discouraged when they first begin meditating because they're looking for a dramatic experience. However, at first, the experience of our true nature is rarely dramatic, but subtle. It may appear as a soft vibration, aliveness, lightheadedness, expansion, relaxation, peace, or contentment. This isn't what we expect our true self, Essence, to feel like. The ego certainly would like and expects something more than this, and it doesn't like to fail at what it tries, so it uses the lack of drama as proof that nothing worthwhile is to be found in meditating. The ego is into instant gratification, and it doesn't find meditation gratifying. On the contrary, meditation leaves the ego disempowered and with nothing to do.

The ego seeks spiritual experience to be special, which is also why it's willing to go along with spiritual seeking. The ego hopes that spirituality will bring it more power—spiritual power. What it doesn't realize is the price to be paid. Once the ego catches on that its own demise, or at least the diminishment of its power, is the goal of spiritual practice, the ego finds ways to subvert that practice while still appearing to be "on the path."

The ego's sabotage of spiritual progress is easy to see in spiritual seekers. They come to spiritual gatherings for spiritual reasons but find ways to walk away with little of real value. They find fault with the teacher, the teachings, the students, the approach, or the techniques. They presume there's nothing there for them, and so there isn't. Some go from teacher to teacher for decades, at once proclaiming their sincerity and their frustration with what is offered and not seeing how perhaps their own ego is the saboteur of their progress and not the teachings, the teacher, or the method.

It's far too easy to find fault with teachers, teachings, and methods, and that is the ego's job in whatever realm it's involved in. The ego analyzes, judges, and evaluates, which is how it maintains its own mental reality and keeps itself separate from real life and not fully engaged in the present moment. This analysis isn't true discrimination, which can only come from Essence. The discrimination of the ego is tainted by its point of view and therefore not discrimination at all. The ego can't see the truth about life because it doesn't have eyes for what is real and true even if it wanted to see it. The ego is the creator of illusion, not the clarifier of reality.

The ego can't discern the truth of spiritual teachings. Only the Heart can discern the truth, and the ego obscures the Heart's understanding. Those who manage to drop into the Heart through spiritual practices or by aligning with a true teacher can discover their true nature; those who don't take longer to find it. But eventually, everyone discovers who they really are. Spiritual evolution can be slowed down by the ego, but it can't be waylaid forever.

By quieting the mind, meditation gives us a chance to experience something other than our thoughts. The mind isn't the only thing here, although that's the way it seems when we're identified with it. Once we withdraw our attention from our thoughts and the imaginary world created by thought, we can begin to experience what else is here in this vastly alive present moment. What we experience when we are fully present in the moment is real life as it is unfolding, Essence, and the qualities of Essence: peace, joy, contentment, acceptance, and love.

Meditation is about *experiencing* instead of thinking. When we're identified with the ego, thinking takes the place of experiencing in most moments. Meditation turns this around. It teaches us to be aware of and present to everything that's happening in the moment, not just aware of our thoughts or feelings. Absorption in thoughts and feelings is the egoic state of consciousness. Meditation helps us move out of that state and into the present moment, where Essence can be experienced.

When we are in the moment instead of absorbed in our thoughts, thinking still happens, but we are aware of much more happening than thinking. We are aware of life, real life, as it is unfolding. Meditation teaches us to notice thoughts and allow them to come and go, but to not identify with them. After sitting in meditation for a while, our thoughts fall into the background, and real life takes the foreground. After practicing meditation regularly for some time, we establish a new relationship to thought, one where thoughts are more permanently in the background, and we are just present to life as it is unfolding in the moment.

To be free of conditioning, thoughts and even feelings don't have to stop, and they're not likely to. We only have to stop believing and responding to our thoughts and feelings, stop identifying with them. Here is a meditation that will help you practice that:

Exercise: Meditating on Thought

A useful meditation for learning to disengage from thoughts and feelings is to simply watch your thoughts arise and disappear. If you catch yourself being involved with a thought, just return to watching your thoughts arise and disappear.

Who is this you that is watching your thoughts? It is the same you that gets involved in the thoughts. This you is either identified with thought or not identified with thought, but the you still exists in either case. The difference is that some level of suffering happens when the you is identified with thought, while peace and happiness happen when the you is not identified with thought. Nothing really changed but identification.

One of the simplest forms of meditation is listening. You don't even have to sit still to practice listening. Except for when we are asleep, listening is always happening; we are either listening to the mind or something else. When we aren't listening to the mind, the opportunity exists to be aware that listening is still happening. Listening is part of Awareness, which is a name that is often given to our true nature. If you look closely at who you really are, you find only Awareness: vast empty space that is aware, conscious. You are this consciousness, this awareness, of the mind, of feelings, of sounds, of sights, of sensations, of energy, of what *is* in any moment. Here is a simple way to meditate to sound:

Exercise: Listening Meditation

You can do this meditation anywhere. Notice the sounds in your environment without thinking about them or commenting on them. If you catch yourself thinking about a sound or something else, gently bring yourself back to listening.

Notice how a sound comes into your awareness and then disappears. Even sounds that continue for a long time are never exactly the same from moment to moment. Every sound is unique and comes freshly out of the moment. You never know what the next sound will be or when it will appear. You never know what combination of sounds will appear. Listening to the sounds that arise from each moment, keeps you noticing and allowing the moment to be just the way it is. Listening firmly plants you in Awareness, which experiences every moment as rich.

Listening aligns us immediately with Awareness, or Essence, because listening is an aspect of it. Awareness is allowing by nature, and listening allows whatever is being heard. Listening puts us in a receptive state that allows whatever is happening. When we are listening, we aren't acting on what is happening, and we don't have an opinion about it. Listening just allows whatever is to be the way it is. Listening can be more than just a meditation; it can be the way we are in every moment. Listening is the opposite of what the mind does with whatever is happening.

Listening in this way is much easier, more peaceful, and keeps us much less busy than listening to the mind. While listening to the mind is wearisome and following the mind is exhausting, listening as a spiritual practice is simple, joyous, and calming. Listening in this way can become a way of being and remaining aligned with Essence. Life can be lived very nicely from this vantage point.

You will find that listening in this way is more like a full-body listening because listening takes place not only through the ears, but also through your entire body, energy field, and beyond. Listening gets us in touch with the Awareness that is paying attention to the present moment. It aligns us with Essence, our true nature.

As you listen and allow yourself to be receptive to whatever is happening in the moment, you can feel the energy of Essence, which is fully at peace and content with the moment. This energy is tangible and feels like a vibration or aliveness. When you feel that aliveness, it means you are aligned with Essence. When that aliveness is absent, you are likely to be aligned, or identified, with something else—the mind. You can use the energetic sensation of aliveness to check to see if you are identified with the mind or with Essence. To align with Essence, all you have to do is listen to, or notice, that aliveness.

The act of noticing, or listening, brings us into the moment, the Now, and the act of allowing keeps us in the Now and aligned with Essence. To remain in the Now, we have to keep saying yes to whatever is happening. Once we land in the Now, the mind tends to come in and reject something about it, which takes us out of the present moment and out of Essence. Allowing is the nature of Essence, so when we allow, we automatically drop into Essence. Allowing doesn't mean being passive in the world, since Essence moves us in whatever ways are necessary as it sees fit.

Exercise: Listening as a Spiritual Practice

You can make listening a spiritual practice by just listening without think-

ing. You can't listen and think at the same time, so if you catch yourself thinking, just bring yourself back to listening. Any judgments, opinions, stories, beliefs, labels, or concepts that arise are the mind coming in. Note these and then return to listening. Just keep coming back to listening and see how doing this transforms your life. Do this practice as often as you can until you become established in Essence in your daily life and your speech and actions reflect that.

Many people also use their breath or movements, such as walking, running, yoga, dancing, or Tai Chi, as a meditation. When we focus our attention on our breath or on physical movements without getting involved in any thoughts, we drop into Essence. When we are focused on our breath, body, or senses without thinking, there's a feeling of oneness with what we're focusing on and a disappearance of the sense of a separate self. We experience the nothingness that we are, and in that experience is also the experience of the every-thingness that we are.

When we're not involved in thinking, and the *me* is out of the way, who we really are manifests as the experience of being both nothing and everything. The *me* is the experience of boundaries or separation between the false self and everything else. Separation is painful because it isn't true that we are actually separate from everything else. When we experience our true nature, we feel oneness and joy, not separation. Joy is a sign that you've found the truth, just as suffering is a sign that you are believing a lie.

PRAYER

Prayer can be a tool for moving from the ego to Essence when we pray for that. Prayers that ask for what the ego wants keep us tied to the illusion that happiness can be found in something external to us. These kinds of prayers aren't useful, but when we are identified with the ego, it's natural to pray for what the ego wants. The ego will try anything that promises to help it get what it wants, even praying. Prayers on behalf of the ego are sometimes answered because there's much to be learned from getting what we want. For one thing, we learn that getting what the ego wants isn't always what it's cracked up to be.

A better use of prayer is to ask for the trust and courage to gracefully deal with whatever life brings us. Trust is especially needed in trying times, when trust can be difficult to access. So we ask for help in trusting and surrendering to whatever we find challenging and difficult to accept.

Beings of light can strengthen our trust and send us insight and inspiration to help us through difficult times. They also send us people and other resources we need. If we trust this, we are more likely to recognize that help when it appears. Trusting opens us up to receiving the Grace and help that is available. Distrust closes us to receiving. Distrust is a lack of belief in Grace and our connection with all that is, and that will be our experience for as long as we hold that belief. Once we change that belief and trust that Grace and help are available, life delivers that. Our beliefs can either open or close the door to Grace.

A prayer can be a carefully composed statement or unspoken but felt. Our intentions and deepest desires are known by those who guide our evolution, and they respond to our intentions and desires as well as to our words. Beings gauge their guidance of us on their experience of our readiness to evolve and receive, and they offer their services accordingly. They can see who is ripe and ready and who isn't. The beings working with you know you well and know how to facilitate your evolution and understanding. When you affirm your willingness to evolve and *feel* the desire for that strongly, this feeling draws helpers to you in great numbers. Although your evolution isn't entirely in your hands, prayer can remove any blocks to your evolution that you may be responsible for.

Prayer is powerful not only because it summons forces who are there to help us, but also because it summons our own will to help ourselves overcome our conditioning and the egoic state of consciousness. Waking up out of the egoic trance requires a will to do that. That will comes from Essence, not from the ego. It is our own will to awaken to our natural state that ultimately awakens us. This will comes from Essence when it's time for us to awaken. Nevertheless, many don't heed the call from Essence to awaken, but choose to stay asleep a little longer. Prayer can firm up our commitment to awakening, which can speed the process along.

FORGIVENESS

A lack of forgiveness keeps us tied to stories about the past. These stories are manufactured by the ego and keep us involved with the egoic mind. They keep us stuck in the past and stuck in a certain image of ourselves that corresponds to that story. As long as we're holding onto a particular self-image, another truer one can't take its place. To have a truer self-image, it's necessary to let go of other self-images because only one self-image can operate at a time.

Stories we have about the past tend to be charged with emotion, or they wouldn't linger as they do. This emotion can make letting go of the self-image difficult because the emotion attached to it makes the story seem so real and true. Emotion has a way of convincing us that the stories we tell about ourselves and our life are true. Some work may be needed to diffuse the emotion before the negative self-image attached to a story can let go and another more positive self-image can take its place.

Forgiveness allows you to let go of the stories that keep you stuck in your particular perceptions and self-image. For example, people who have a story of victimization often see themselves as victims. They form an identity and self-image that includes the experience of victimization, and that identity determines to some extent how they respond to life. These self-images often become self-fulfilling prophecies, which draw to us similar experiences. "Victims" are often victimized more than once, and "failures" often fail more than once. Essence allows us to experience the results of having a particular self-image until we decide to become free of it. Forgiveness allows us to move on from what happened in the past and begin to see ourselves differently.

Your perceptions are just that—your perceptions. They are true to you, but only true to you. No story can ever be true because it doesn't reflect enough of the truth. Given that, your particular perceptions aren't valuable or useful. Your perceptions only tell you about your conditioning, since they are determined by your conditioning. Therefore, examining your stories for what they reveal about your conditioning can be useful, but in and of themselves, your particular perception of the past has no value or ultimate truth.

Forgiveness is difficult because it requires humbling. Acknowledging that our perceptions are not the truth and that they keep us from what we really want—happiness, love, peace, and joy—is humbling. We can't have our stories about the past *and* be happy. These stories don't make us happy, but are the source of unhappiness. We think that events rob us of our happiness, when in fact, we rob ourselves of happiness by telling ourselves a story about an event that makes us unhappy and keeps us stuck in negative thoughts and feelings.

Forgiveness frees us from this prison of negativity by giving us a way out of our story. You forgive whatever you or someone else did so that you can be here, now, in the present moment instead of in thoughts and feelings related to some other moment in the past. Here is an exercise that will help you forgive:

Exercise: Forgiveness

Forgiveness begins with a simple statement, or affirmation, to forgive: "I forgive...." This affirmation will have to be repeated whenever thoughts or feelings arise about the past. When that happens, you immediately replace those thoughts with the affirmation, "I forgive...." Doing this will eventually reprogram your thoughts, and the negative emotions connected to those thoughts will eventually dissipate. This sounds simple, but being diligent about this can be difficult when the thoughts and feelings have become very strong.

There's really no other way out of certain painful feelings than doing this work. Calling on beings of light to help you forgive and heal will help, but you have to make a commitment to doing the work around forgiveness for yourself. If you continue to dwell on negative (untrue) stories about the past and feed your negative emotions, those feelings will become stronger. The only way out of this suffering is to do the opposite: Don't give those thoughts and feelings your attention, and put your attention on what's good and beautiful in the present moment. Forgiveness gets you out of the trap created by the negative mind, but you have to commit yourself to forgiveness as strongly as you committed yourself to your thoughts about the past.

GRATITUDE

Gratitude comes from Essence. It's not the ego's nature to be grateful, but quite the opposite. When you are feeling gratitude, it's helpful to acknowledge it and really allow yourself to feel it, and then sustain it by expressing it. Essence is in love with all of life and bursting with joy over the miracle that is life. The ego dampens this joy with complaints and ideas about how things could be better. We rarely stay long in gratitude because the ego is so quick to pull us out of it with a thought. But if we can learn to give our attention to the ever-present gratitude that arises from Essence instead of our thoughts, gratitude can become our ongoing state.

We are programmed to pay attention to the ego and its complaints. To counteract this, we have to give our attention to gratitude when it's there and create it when it's not there by noticing what is good and lovable about life instead of what we don't like. The ego's commentary is often about what is wrong with something or lacking in the moment. If we give our attention to the ego's negativity, then that will be our experience and what we give voice to. On the other hand, if we notice the experience our true self is having instead of the mind's running commentary, we will experience life as good and feel gratitude.

The experience of Essence is one of love, acceptance, and openness to all life. This experience is ongoing and accessible in any moment; it just isn't experienced through the mind. To be happy and feel the joy of Essence, we have to turn away from the mind to the experience of the moment, where that joy can be felt. Joy is an *experience*, not a thought, and it is only available in the here and now. You have to discover joy in the moment. Once you do, you have to continue to give joy your attention, or you're likely to find yourself thinking again. Being in Essence and staying there requires our continued attention to the moment rather than to the mind. Whenever our attention wavers from what is happening in the present moment, we'll be back in the mind.

Whatever we give our attention to becomes stronger, so if you give your attention to what you are *not* grateful for, feelings of lack, resentment, anger, disappointment, and frustration will grow. On the other hand, if you give your attention to what you *are* grateful for, the feeling of gratitude grows along with other positive feelings: joy, peace, contentment, acceptance, and happiness. Here is an exercise that will increase your feelings of gratitude:

Exercise: Increasing Gratitude

You can train yourself to be more aware and expressive of gratitude in any number of ways:

1. *Write down all the things you are grateful for and recite them to yourself every morning and night.*

2. *Make a collage or picture of everything you are grateful for. This is a very powerful way of expressing and reinforcing your gratitude because making a collage or picture takes time, energy, and focus.*

3. *Bring gratitude to as many moments as possible during your day.*

Doing these things to align yourself with gratitude rather than lack is a very powerful spiritual practice that can change your life when done consistently.

The reason gratitude can change your life is that it is a simple way to move from the ego to Essence. All it requires is remembering to be grateful. You can reprogram your mind by using gratitude to replace any thought of lack, resentment, disappointment, frustration, or anger. Whenever a negative thought arises, replace it with gratitude. For example, if the thought arises, "He shouldn't have done that to me," it can be replaced with, "I'm grateful I have the strength and understanding to deal with this." In doing this, you move from victimization to peace, personal power, and acceptance.

Statements of gratitude such as this are truer than negative stories, and they eliminate the suffering caused by our stories. We have the power to change our experience of life by changing what we tell ourselves about your experiences. Our initial response to any experience is likely to come from the ego because it's programmed to respond instantly, automatically, defensively, and negatively to whatever is happening. We have to learn to slow down our responses enough to allow for a different, more positive response. When we do that, we are reprogramming our mind and healing our conditioning, and that conditioning is less likely to arise again, or arise as strongly.

Because the egoic mind is so unrelentingly negative and because we are programmed to listen to it, we have to be unrelentingly committed to another, more positive perspective, or we'll be left with the egoic mind's perspective. Happiness doesn't lie in the direction of negativity. No matter how wronged we may feel by someone or by life, the only way out of that suffering is to change our perception of the situation. Essence is grateful for every experience because every experience brings growth and learning and because certain attributes, such as compassion, patience, and perseverance, can only be developed through challenges. Here is an exercise that will help you feel grateful for your challenges:

Exercise: Being Grateful for Challenges

Although it may not be possible to be grateful for having had a particular experience, we can learn to focus on being grateful for the growth or other positive things that came from it. No experience is without benefit. These benefits may be difficult to see when we are in the midst of a particular tragedy, but as time passes, seeing the growth and other benefits becomes easier.

Ask yourself: How did that experience serve me? What was good about it? How have I grown as a result of it? How has my life changed for the better? The more you can focus on how something served you, the easier it will be to forgive, let go, and move on.

We tend to focus on what we dislike about something, how awful it is, and how unfair it is, and other people are often happy to agree with us and reinforce this perspective. However, focusing on the negative is not healing and it doesn't help us grow from the experience and turn it into the gold that it can be. Every difficult experience can be transmuted and be a means of transformation of ourselves and others, or it can be a source of ongoing pain and limitation. We get to choose what the result of an experience will be. Gratitude is the key to shifting our perspective to one that will heal us and help us grow and be a positive force in the world.

THE WILLINGNESS TO NOT KNOW

No one likes a know-it-all, but that is what everyone's egoic mind is. The mind pretends to know things it doesn't know and even things it can't know, because not knowing is anathema to it. Wanting to know something when it is impossible to is just one more way the ego struggles against life. Life is a mystery. There are many more things we don't know than we do. The ego doesn't like this, and its way of coping with that unpleasant fact is to pretend to know. Pretending to know when we don't is a lie, and it takes us away from the truth: We don't know. Wanting to know, trying to know, and pretending to know keep us tied to the egoic mind and out of touch with the alive, present moment that vibrates in wonderment: What will happen next? No one really knows.

The only one who really cares what will happen next is the ego, because Essence is open to having any experience and loves life's unpredictability. The ego spends so much time concerned with what will happen (and with what has happened) that it misses out on what is happening right now, which is constantly changing. Life is rich when it's just experienced, but when the experience of the moment gets clouded by thoughts about the past, present, and future, life loses its juiciness and aliveness. This lack of aliveness feels like a problem that needs to be solved, so the ego tries to solve it by going after things it thinks will make life juicier. But things just can't deliver the juiciness of the experience of real life, of our true nature. The ego's state of discontentment is a state of dis-ease, which needs to be healed, and one of the solutions is in being willing to not know.

Whenever we catch the egoic mind at its game of pretending to know and we realize we really don't know, we drop into Essence, where not knowing feels rich and peaceful. Knowing promises to deliver everything the ego wants, which is why it sees knowing as so desirable, but being willing to not know is actually what delivers everything we have ever really wanted. This is because when we admit we don't know, the opinions, judgments, and perspectives the ego holds so dear collapse. They can't be maintained in the face of the truth: We don't know. The only way they can be maintained is if we believe they are true. Once they are seen as having no real truth, we stop identifying with them and the false self and immediately drop into Essence, where the peace and love we really want can be experienced.

What if your opinions were not yours? Would you still respect them so much? We tend to believe our opinions just because they are ours, without really examining them. One opinion is no more valid or real than another. Opinions are not facts, but we relate to our opinions as if they were true, meaningful, and important. Here is an exercise that will help you examine your opinions:

Exercise: Examining Your Opinions

Make a list of some of your opinions and then ask, "Is that really true?"

For every opinion you hold, you will probably find that you also hold a contradictory one. This is true of your likes and dislikes as well. For example, if you say, "I like chocolate," is it also true that sometimes you don't like it—like when it stains your clothes, makes you feel sick, or makes you fat? There's hardly an opinion, preference, judgment, or belief you hold that is always true for you, and yet we hold them as if they were.

The egoic mind isn't consistent in what it believes, but it is consistent in believing whatever it believes. The egoic mind doesn't withstand scrutiny very well. Once you begin to question the beliefs and opinions you hold dear, you realize how insubstantial they are and how much energy you've invested in thinking about them, talking about them, and defending them. Opinions just aren't worth that much energy. Admitting we don't know frees up our energy to pay attention to what is happening now and what is true now.

The problem with opinions is that they aren't connected to *now*, but to some other point in time when they were formed. They may have been true once, but are they true now? Because opinions aren't very true and they don't hold up over time, they aren't worth hanging our identity on. When we finally admit we don't know, it frees up our energy to look and see what is true *now.* Is there an opinion, preference, or belief arising now? Is it true? What can you say about what is arising now that *is* true? If a bird is singing now, we can say that that is true now; however, it may not be true in a few seconds. What do you actually, really know right now?

When you ask yourself this question, you discover that you don't know very much, and that's the truth. Fortunately, it isn't necessary to know anything more than what you know right now. Knowing is actually highly overrated. Outside of knowledge that is functional, knowing isn't that useful because most of what we think we know (beyond facts) isn't true anyway. You know how to operate a car, which is functional knowledge, but do you know how you will feel about your car next week or even tomorrow? We pretend we do. We pretend that however we feel about something right now is how we feel and will always feel. We pretend that our opinions about our car or cars in general or anything else will be the same tomorrow, but we don't know that. We don't even know if we'll have a car tomorrow, but we pretend we will. We make a lot of assumptions about how life will be based on how life is right now and on how we feel about life right now, but we have no way of knowing what the next minute will be like, much less tomorrow or next year.

Not buying into the egoic mind's insistence that it knows more than it does frees us from the mind and drops us into Essence, where there's no longer a need to know, nor all the striving and defending that go with that. Tremendous amounts of energy are expended in trying to know and in defending that knowing, which could be put to better use. Just being and allowing life to be as it is without having to know or figure it out is what frees us from the relentless striving of the ego to control life and make life fit its ideas and desires.

To be free, we have to be willing to not know. We have to be humble enough to allow ourselves to not know and courageous enough to trust that not knowing is the natural state and that within that state is everything we've been looking for. If you lose your opinions, you will not have lost anything, and you will have gained everything that really matters.

BEING PRESENT

Healing our conditioning requires being present to our thoughts instead of responding automatically to them, which is what happens when we are identified with our egoic mind. Essence is what is able to be present to conditioning, to be *aware* of it and compassionate toward it. When we bring awareness, which is a quality of Essence, to our conditioning, our conditioning can be seen for what it is, understood, and released. On the other hand, when we identify with and act out our conditioning, we reinforce and strengthen it. Here is an exercise that will help make you more aware of Awareness, which is another word for Essence:

Exercise: Noticing Awareness

Fortunately, we all have access to Awareness because it is ever-present and who we really are. No matter how identified you are with the ego, you still have access to your true nature through the simple act of noticing. What is noticing you reading these words right now? What is noticing your thoughts about what you are reading? What is noticing and experiencing this mo-

ment? That is Awareness, your true nature.

When we bring Awareness to any thought or feeling, it will heal it, that is, it will show us how little truth that thought or feeling has. Awareness has the power to break our identification with the ego. When we become aware that we are Aware, we are in Essence and no longer identified with the ego. Becoming aware of what is Aware puts us in a different relationship to ourselves and life, one in which we are free to respond naturally and spontaneously to what the moment calls for instead of from our conditioned ideas and beliefs. This is a remarkable and life-altering shift, this simple shift to being aware of ourselves as Awareness. Moving from the ego to Essence is simply a shift of attention away from thought onto what is *aware* of thought.

From Awareness, or Essence, life is simple and sweet. It is simple because it is uncomplicated by analysis or plans about what to do next. When we are fully in the present moment and in Essence, spontaneous urges arise to do what is appropriate in the moment. And in the next moment, whatever is appropriate to do or not do arises. We never know what that will be from one moment to the next, but we can trust it. The egoic mind busies itself with plans about what to do in the present moment and in moments to come, which the ego assumes or hopes will look a certain way. Planning for these moments is useless because they don't exist and won't ever exist as we imagine them. When an urge to plan comes from Essence, it arises spontaneously, and the plan is held lightly, with the understanding that it could change at any time.

This shift from the ego to Essence is a shift in the importance of thought and our relationship to it. When we are identified with the ego, our thoughts determine what we do and how we feel. They shape our life and determine our experience of life. Once we move into Awareness of thought rather than identification with it, this changes. Thought is just one thing that is happening within Awareness and by no means the main shaper of life and our experience of life.

When thought, or conditioning, is no longer the main driver and shaper of our life, it becomes clear that something else is driving and shaping life, and it's doing a beautiful job. Who you really are has been living and experiencing your life all along, and it has allowed thought to drive you, while it has also inserted itself into your life, steering you and guiding you according to its intentions. It turns out that thought was never as necessary as you thought! If fact, we function much better without most thoughts. Freedom is freedom from thoughts as drivers and shapers of life. Our thoughts were never meant to guide our life. Thinking is useful for practical purposes, but our conditioning isn't a good guide for how to live. In fact, it's a poor guide and creates all sorts of difficulties and pain.

We are all programmed to allow thoughts to determine our actions and experience. Once we see that they don't need to and that something else is a more worthy guide, we can begin the work of freeing ourselves from our negative conditioning, which keeps us tethered to the ego.

Something else is here living this life, and it has always been here. It is beautiful, simple, and free. Once you see that that is who you are, you don't have to go back to the ego. It served its role. Through the suffering it caused, it brought you to a place of no suffering; it brought you home to Essence. The ego served perfectly.

There comes a point in everyone's evolution when it's time to serve life from Essence, with all the wisdom that has been gained. Healing your conditioning is not something you do for yourself, but something you do for your Self in all the many human guises you appear in. Once you are free, that is the beginning of a whole new adventure and relationship to life, one in which love, not fear, prevails, and service to the rest of your Self is the driving force.

ABOUT THE AUTHOR

Gina Lake is a spiritual teacher who is devoted to helping others wake up and live in the moment through counseling, intensives, and her books. She has a masters degree in counseling psychology and over twenty years experience supporting people in their spiritual growth. Her books include *Radical Happiness, Embracing the Now, Anatomy of Desire, Return to Essence, What About Now? Loving in the Moment, Living in the Now,* and *Getting Free.* Her website offers information about her books and consultations, free e-books, book excerpts, a free monthly newsletter, a blog, and audio and video recordings: *www.radicalhappiness.com.*